Awesome
REAL-LIFE
BIBLE DEVOTIONS
for kids

This book belongs to

Hope E. Anderson

Presented by

Daddy + Mommy

Date

Christmas 1999

Edited by Jeannie Harmon

Scripture text from the International Children's Bible
New Century Version

Chariot Books™
David C. Cook Publishing Co.

Published by Chariot Books™,
an imprint of Chariot Family Products
David C. Cook Publishing Co., Elgin, Illinois 60120
David C. Cook Publishing Co., Weston, Ontario
Nova Distribution Ltd., Torquay, England

AWESOME REAL-LIFE BIBLE DEVOTIONS FOR KIDS

Edited by Jeannie Harmon
Cover design by Elizabeth Thompson
Internal design/production by Paul Mouw, Mouw and Associates, Glen Ellyn, Il.

First Printing, 1991
Printed in the United States of America
95 94   5 4 3

Library of Congress Cataloging-in-Publication Data

Awesome Real-Life Bible Devotions For Kids / edited by Jeannie Harmon.
Scripture text taken from the *International Children's Bible,* New Century Version.
Summary: A devotion book containing Bible readings, art, prayers, questions, and space for
personal journal entries.
ISBN 1-55513-737-7
1. Children — Prayer-books and devotionals — English. [1. Prayer books and devotions.] I.
Harmon, Jeannie. II Chariot Books. BV4870.A94 1991
242'.62—dc20   91-182.15

Thanks to the team that made this book possible:
Barbara Nagle, Cathy Davis, Brian Reck, Jeannie Harmon, Steve Johnson,
Sue Leaf, Paul Mouw, Julie Smith

What's in This Book?

Devotions from the Old Testament

Devotions from the New Testament

SPENDING time with God is a totally awesome addition to any day. Most of us, though, don't know how to have devotions or pray or understand the Bible. It's all so confusing.

Awesome Real-Life Devotions for Kids is the answer to the problem. Everything you need is right here. We'll take you through the Old and New Testaments in a fun way, breaking them into bite-size pieces so that you'll understand God's Word, get some direction on how He wants you to live, and get some good ideas on how to put all this into practice.

Each devotion is two or three pages long and chock full of exciting things to look at and read. Look for these special features:

• **Character Value Box:** The key idea for each devotion is shown in a black box. This tells you what the main theme will be for that devotion. It's a principle from God's Word to help you strengthen your relationship with God, others, and yourself.

Confidence

• **Bible Stories:** All Bible stories are taken from the *International Children's Bible,* an easy-to-understand version of God's Word for kids like you. Look for the large bold type and you'll know that the story begins here.

THEN the Lord God took dust from the ground and formed man from it. The Lord breathed the breath of life into the man's nose. And the man became a living person. . . .

¹⁵The Lord God put the man in the garden of Eden to care for it and work it. . . .

¹⁸Then the Lord God said, "It is not good for the man to be alone. I will make a helper who is right for him."

¹⁹From the ground God formed

WHERE'S YOUR COURAGE, MEN? AND YOUR FAITH IN GOD?

THERE'S ONLY ONE WAY TO STOP JOSHUA'S WILD TALK!

• **Pictures:** Each devotion will come alive with colorful illustrations taken from *The Picture Bible*. A story is always easier to understand if you have pictures to give you a feel for what is going on.

• **Key Verse:** Each devotion has a key verse that will help you develop the character trait given in that day's devotion. You will want to learn these verses by memory so that when you need help, God's Words will be in your mind to help you through the situation.

Remain in me a follow my teach you do this, th can ask for anything and it will be given

• **Something To Think About:** These questions and ideas will help you to think about situations in your own life that might be similar to those in the Bible story.

? God created a beautiful place f animals to have fun with, and p Everything he needed, right? So v

? Was God able to take care of A do it?

? Think of one area where you nee need help with choosing friends and to the teacher on time, or reso

• **Prayer:** Each devotion has a short prayer to get you started talking to God. Begin by reading the prayer with your devotion. You'll find that talking to God can be like talking to your best friend. You'll want to add your own words to tell God other important things that are going on in your life.

Thanks, God, for giving me the promise the Bible that if I lieve in You, You'll help me when I need help. I put my confidence in You. Amen.

• **Journal entry:** This special space is for you to think of ideas of how you can apply the main idea of the devotion to your everyday life. Each journal entry is different from the one before, so you'll have many opportunities to be creative!

DRAW A PICT IN YOUR LIFE LOUD WHAT Y HELP YOU WITH JUST AS YOU

We've given you everything you need to get started. Now, it's up to you! You can read one every day, or one a week, or whenever you choose. We're sure that you'll discover that getting into God's Word can be an awesome experience! . . . Not only for today, but for every day throughout your life.

*HIS JEWISH NAME IS SAUL.

You are young, . . .
but do not let anyone treat you as if you were not important.
Be an example to show the believers how they should live.
Show them . . .
with your words,
with the way you live,
with your love,
with your faith,
and with your pure life.

I Timothy 4:12

Adam Needed Help!

IN THE BEGINNING, GOD CREATED
EVERYTHING. EACH DAY FOR SIX
DAYS HE ADDED SOMETHING
TO MAKE THE WORLD MORE
COMPLETE. HIS CREATION
PLAN WAS:

DAY 1--HEAVEN AND EARTH
LIGHT AND DARKNESS
DAY AND NIGHT
DAY 2--SKY AND CLOUDS
DAY 3--EARTH AND SEAS
TREES, PLANTS,
FRUITS, AND
FLOWERS
DAY 4--SUN, MOON,
AND STARS,
THE SEASONS
DAY 5--FISH
AND
BIRDS
DAY 6--ANIMALS
FIRST MAN
AND FIRST
WOMAN
ON THE SEVENTH DAY,
GOD RESTED.
GOD TOLD ADAM
THAT IT WAS HIS
JOB TO NAME ALL
THE ANIMALS AND
TEND THE GARDEN OF
EDEN. TAKING CARE OF
ALL OF THIS WAS A BIG
JOB. HE NEEDED HELP! . . .

Morell

THEN the Lord God took dust from the ground and formed man from it.

The Lord breathed the breath of life into the man's nose. And the man became a living person. . . .

15The Lord God put the man in the garden of Eden to care for it and work it. . . .

18Then the Lord God said, "It is not good for the man to be alone. I will make a helper who is right for him."

19From the ground God formed every wild animal and every bird in the sky. He brought them to the man so the man could name them. Whatever the man called each living thing, that became its name. 20The man gave names to all the tame animals, to the birds in the sky and to all the wild animals. But Adam did not find a helper that was right for him. 21So the Lord God caused the man to sleep very deeply. While the man was asleep, God took one of the ribs from the man's body. Then God closed the man's skin at the place where he took the rib. 22The Lord God used the rib from the man to make a woman. Then the Lord brought the woman to the man.

23And the man said,
"Now, this is someone whose bones came from my bones.
Her body came from my body.
I will call her 'woman,'
because she was taken out of man."

From Genesis 2

?God created a beautiful place for Adam to live, lots of animals to have fun with, and plenty of good things to eat. Everything he needed, right? So why did Adam still need help?

?Was God able to take care of Adam's problem? How did He do it?

?Think of one area where you need God's help. Perhaps you need help with choosing friends, getting your homework done and to the teacher on time, or resolving a problem in your family.

> Remain in me and follow my teachings. If you do this, then you can ask for anything you want, and it will be given to you.
>
> John 15:7

Thanks, God, for giving me the promise in the Bible that if I believe in You, You'll help me when I need help. I put my confidence in You. Amen.

DRAW A PICTURE OF ONE NEED THAT YOU HAVE IN YOUR LIFE TODAY. THEN TELL GOD OUT LOUD WHAT YOUR NEED IS AND ASK HIM TO HELP YOU WITH THE SITUATION. TALK TO GOD JUST AS YOU TALK TO YOUR BEST FRIEND.

Who Me? . . . . It Wasn't My Fault!

GOD TOOK ADAM AND EVE TO THE GARDEN OF EDEN AND SHOWED THEM THE BEAUTY AND FRUITFULNESS OF IT. GOD COMMANDED, "YOU MUST NOT EAT FRUIT FROM THE TREE THAT IS IN THE MIDDLE OF THE GARDEN. YOU MUST NOT EVEN TOUCH IT, OR YOU WILL DIE."

NOW the snake was the most clever of all the wild animals the Lord God had made. One day the snake spoke to the woman. He said, "Did God really say that you must not eat fruit from any tree in the garden?" 2 The woman answered . . . "God told us, 'You must not eat fruit from the tree that is in the middle of the garden. . . . or you will die.'" 4 But the snake said to the woman, "You will not die. 5 God knows that if you eat the fruit from that tree, you will learn about good and evil. Then you will be like God!" 6 The woman saw that the tree was beautiful. She saw that its fruit was good to eat and that it would make her wise. So she took some of its fruit and ate it. She also gave some of the fruit to her husband, and he ate it. . . . 7 Then, it was as if the man's and the woman's eyes were opened. . . . 8 Then they heard the Lord God walking in the garden . . . during the cool part of the day. And the man and his wife hid from the Lord God among the trees in the garden. 9 But the Lord God called to the man. The Lord said, "Where are you?" 10 The man answered, "I heard you walking in the garden. I was afraid. . . . So I hid." 11 God said to the man, " . . . Did you eat fruit from that tree? I commanded you not to eat from that tree." 12 The man said, "You gave this woman to me. She gave me fruit from the tree. So I ate it." 13 Then the Lord God said to the woman, "What have you done?" She answered, "The snake tricked me. So I ate the fruit."

From Genesis 3

12

?What lie did the snake tell Eve? Did she believe the lie?

?How did she get Adam involved? When God asked them about eating the fruit, what did Adam and Eve tell God?

?All of us do things we shouldn't. Sometimes we choose to make bad choices; sometimes we don't plan on doing wrong, it just happens. In either case, we need to be honest enough to say, "I did wrong. I'm sorry."

AFRAID!

QUICK—LET'S HIDE!

God, examine me and know my heart. Test me and know my thoughts. See if there is any bad thing in me. Lead me in the way you set long ago.

Psalm 139:23, 24

Prayer: Thank You, God, for loving me even when I don't always make right choices. Help me to be honest enough to say "I'm sorry" when I'm wrong. Thanks for listening.
Amen.

BECAUSE ADAM AND EVE DISOBEYED GOD, GOD TOLD EVE THAT SHE WOULD HAVE GREAT PAIN WHEN SHE DELIVERED A BABY AND THAT HER HUSBAND WOULD RULE OVER HER. HE TOLD ADAM HE WOULD HAVE TO SWEAT AND WORK HARD TO GET FOOD, AND LATER WHEN HE DIED, HIS BODY WOULD GO BACK TO DUST. ADAM AND EVE ALSO HAD TO LEAVE THE BEAUTIFUL GARDEN. GOD PUT ANGELS AND A FLAMING SWORD AT THE ENTRANCE TO KEEP THEM OUT. THE RESULTS OF SIN ARE ALWAYS BAD.

THINK OF A BAD CHOICE YOU MADE THIS WEEK. MAYBE YOU HURT SOMEONE'S FEELINGS, BORROWED SOMETHING YOU SHOULDN'T HAVE, OR SAID SOMETHING THAT WAS ONLY HALF TRUE. HOW DOES THINKING ABOUT THAT TIME MAKE YOU FEEL RIGHT NOW? WRITE A SHORT NOTE TO GOD TELLING HIM HOW YOU FEEL AND WHAT YOU PLAN TO DO TO MAKE THINGS RIGHT.

DEAR GOD,

LOVE,

14

Anger!!!

ADAM AND EVE HAD TWO BOYS, CAIN AND ABEL. AS THEY GREW UP, ABEL TOOK CARE OF THE SHEEP AND CAIN BECAME A FARMER. WHEN IT WAS TIME TO GIVE A SACRIFICE TO THE LORD . . .

CAIN brought a gift to God. He brought some food from the ground. 4Abel brought the best parts of his best sheep. The Lord accepted Abel and his gift. 5But God did not accept Cain and his gift. Cain became very angry and looked unhappy.

6The Lord asked Cain, "Why are you angry? Why do you look so unhappy? 7If you do good, I will accept you. But if you do not do good, sin is already to attack you. Sin wants you. But you must rule over it."

8Cain said to his brother Abel, "Let's go out into the field." So Cain and Abel went into the field. Then Cain attacked his brother Abel and killed him.

9Later, the Lord said to Cain, "Where is your brother Abel?"

Cain answered, "I don't know. Is it my job to take care of my brother?"

10Then the Lord said, "What have you done? Your brother's blood is on the ground. That blood is like a voice that tells me what happened. 11And now you will be cursed in your work with the ground. It is the same ground where your brother's blood fell. Your hands killed him. 12 You will work the ground. But it will not grow good crops for you anymore. You will wander around on the earth."

From Genesis 4

? What do you think God meant when He told Cain that he must "rule over" being tempted to commit sin? Did Cain have a choice whether or not to kill his brother?

? Self-discipline is the willingness to correct or control yourself in order to make yourself a better person. Was Cain self-disciplined? How could he have changed the story's sad ending?

? Most of the time we don't say to ourselves, "I'm going to murder my brother." Usually sin starts as a small seed — such as Cain's being jealous because Abel's gift was accepted. Cain's out-of-control anger grew until he committed murder. Do you have an area in your life where you feel things are getting out of control?

More!▯▯▯➡

Prayer: Dear God, sometimes I'm not very disciplined and don't do what Your Word tells me to do. Remind me when I'm in confusing situations to act as You would act, and say what You would say. Amen.

WHAT IS AN AREA OF YOUR LIFE WHERE YOU THINK THINGS ARE GETTING OUT OF CONTROL? SOME EXAMPLES ARE: YOU'RE NOT GETTING ALONG WITH SOMEONE IN CLASS, HOMEWORK IS NOT TURNED IN ON TIME, YOU'RE ARGUING MORE WITH MOM OR DAD LATELY, ETC. WRITE DOWN ONE THING YOU COULD DO TO HELP THE SITUATION.

MY PROBLEM IS: _____

ONE THING I COULD DO TO HELP MAKE THE SITUATION BETTER IS: _____

YOU AND YOUR BEST FRIEND ARE ENTERING DIFFERENT PROJECTS IN YOUR SCHOOL'S SCIENCE FAIR. EVERYONE LOVES HIS PROJECT, INCLUDING THE TEACHER (WHO USED TO BE YOUR FAVORITE TEACHER!). NO ONE GIVES YOUR PROJECT EVEN A SECOND GLANCE. YOU KNOW IT WON'T WIN ANY PRIZES. WHAT IS ONE THING THAT YOU COULD DO TO STOP THIS INCIDENT FROM RUINING YOUR FRIENDSHIP?

Lord, You Want Me to Build What?

PEOPLE ON THE EARTH
WERE VERY WICKED. VIOLENCE WAS
EVERYWHERE. GOD BECAME SORRY
THAT HE MADE HUMAN BEINGS AND
DECIDED TO DESTROY
EVERY
LIVING
THING,
EXCEPT FOR
NOAH. NOAH
WALKED
WITH GOD
AND WAS A
GOOD MAN.
GOD TOLD HIM

"**BUILD** a boat of cypress wood for yourself.** Make rooms in it and cover it inside and outside with tar. 15This is how big I want you to build the boat: 450 feet long, 75 feet wide and 45 feet high. 16Make an opening around the top of the boat. Make it 18 inches high from the edge of the roof down. Put a door in the side of the boat. Make an upper, middle and lower deck in it. 17I will bring a flood of water on the earth. I will destroy all living things that live under the sky. This includes everything that has the breath of life. Everything on the earth will die. 18But I will make an agreement with you. You, your sons, your wife and your sons' wives will all go into the boat. 19Also, you must bring into the boat two of every living thing, male and female. Keep them alive with you. 20There will be two of every kind of bird, animal and crawling thing. They will come to you to be kept alive. 21Also gather some of every kind of food. Store it on the boat as food for you and the animals."
22Noah did everything that God commanded him.

Morelll➡️

From Genesis 6

? This must have seemed like a strange request to Noah—build a big boat for you, your family, and animals from all over the world! Yet Noah obeyed. What questions might Noah have asked God about the job he was asked to do?

? Noah probably did not fully understand what lay ahead, yet he obeyed without complaining. He could have said, "No way, God. I'm not into boat making." What could have happened if Noah had chosen not to obey God? What would have happened to his family?

? Imagine that you are the captain of a sports team at school and one of the players decides not to obey your instructions. What could happen?

Help me understand, so I can obey your teachings. I will obey them with all my heart.
Ps. 119:34

Dear Lord, help me to be obedient to those who You've placed over me. Help me to understand that they are helping me to become more like You in my actions. Amen.

SOMETIMES IT'S HARD FOR US TO OBEY A PARENT OR A TEACHER. WE DON'T SEE PROBLEMS THAT COULD COME UP DOWN THE LINE AS A RESULT OF OUR CHOOSING NOT TO OBEY. THINK OF ONE AREA WHERE IT IS HARD FOR YOU TO OBEY (KEEPING YOUR ROOM CLEAN, DOING HOMEWORK, NOT FIGHTING WITH YOUR BROTHER OR SISTER, ETC.). THEN ANSWER THE FOLLOWING:

I HAVE TROUBLE OBEYING WHEN:

IF I OBEY, THIS IS WHAT HAPPENS:

IF I DON'T OBEY, THIS IS WHAT HAPPENS:

TALK TO GOD ABOUT YOUR CHOICES AND PLAN TO BE OBEDIENT NEXT TIME WITH HIS HELP.

The Only Boat in the Whole World

WHEN ALL THE ANIMALS WERE GATHERED TO THE ARK AND NOAH AND HIS FAMILY WERE INSIDE, GOD SHUT THE DOOR. RAIN FELL FOR FORTY DAYS AND FORTY NIGHTS. ALL THE EARTH WAS COVERED WITH WATER.

LOOK! THE GREAT DOOR OF NOAH'S ARK IS CLOSING!

YES...IT SHUT BY INVISI HAN

? Noah, his family, and all the animals were in a boat—the only boat in the entire world. They had no place to land because everything was covered with water. What are some things that Noah might have been afraid of during this time?

? Noah must have felt that God was taking a long time to clear away the water. What could Noah learn while he waited in the boat?

? Sometimes waiting is scary because we don't know how things are going to work out. What is an answer from God you are waiting for?

WATER flooded the earth for 40 days.

As the water rose, it lifted the boat off the ground. ¹⁸The water continued to rise, and the boat floated on the water above the earth. ¹⁹The water rose so much that even the highest mountains under the sky were covered by it. ²⁰The water continued to rise until it was more than 20 feet above the mountains. . . . ²⁴And the waters continued to cover the earth for 150 days.

Chapter 8But God remembered Noah and all the wild animals and tame animals with him in the boat. God made a wind blow over the earth. And the water went down. ²The underground springs stopped flowing. And the clouds in the sky stopped pouring down rain. ³⁻⁴The water that covered the earth began to go down. After 150 days the water had gone down so much that the boat touched land again. It came to rest on one of the mountains of Ararat. This was on the seventeenth day of the seventh month. ⁵The water continued to go down. By the first day of the tenth month the tops of the mountains could be seen.

AN OLIVE BRANCH! THAT MEANS SOME LAND MUST BE DRY AGAIN.

⁶Forty days later Noah opened the window he had made in the boat. ⁷He sent out a raven. It flew here and there until the water had dried up from the earth. ⁸Then Noah sent out a dove. This was to find out if the water had dried up from the ground. ⁹The dove could not find a place to land because water still covered the earth. So it came back to the boat. Noah reached out his hand and took the bird. And he brought it back into the boat.

¹⁰After seven days Noah again sent out the dove from the boat. ¹¹And that evening it came back to him with a fresh olive leaf in its mouth. Then Noah knew that the ground was almost dry. ¹²Seven days later he sent the dove out again. But this time it did not come back.

From Genesis 7, 8

If we see what we are waiting for, then that is not really hope. People do not hope for something they already have. But we are hoping for something that we do not have yet. We are waiting for it patiently.

Romans 8:24b, 25

Lord, thank You for knowing what is best for me. Help me to be patient and wait for things to happen when You want them to. Amen.

Morel

DRAW
AN
OUTLINE
OF A
BOAT. ON
THE INSIDE
OF YOUR
BOAT WRITE
ONE PROBLEM
THAT YOU WOULD
LIKE GOD TO
ANSWER FOR YOU.
THEN TALK TO HIM
ABOUT IT.

THEN God said to Noah, [16]**"You and your wife, your sons and their wives should go out of the boat.** [17]Bring every animal out of the boat with you—the birds, animals and everything that crawls on the earth. Let them have many young ones and let them grow in number."

[20]. . .Then Noah built an altar to the Lord. Noah took some of all the clean birds and animals. And he burned them on the altar as offerings to God. [21]The Lord was pleased with these sacrifices. He said to himself, "I will never again curse the ground because of human beings. Their thoughts are evil even when they are young. But I will never again destroy every living thing on the earth as I did this time.

Chapter 9And God said, "I am making an agreement between me and you and every living creature that is with you. It will continue from now on. This is the sign: [13]I am putting my rainbow in the clouds. . . . [14]When I bring clouds over the earth, a rainbow appears in the clouds. [15]Then I will remember my agreement. It is between me and you and every living thing. Floodwaters will never again destroy all life on the earth.

WHEN YOU GET AN
ANSWER, WRITE THE
DATE HERE.

From Genesis 8, 9

The Promise of a Rainbow

AS SOON AS NOAH LEAVES THE ARK, HE BUILDS AN ALTAR. HERE HE THANKS GOD FOR HIS CARE AND ASKS GOD'S GUIDANCE IN HELPING NOAH AND HIS FAMILY TO MAKE A NEW START. THEN GOD MAKES A PROMISE TO NOAH AND TO ALL HIS CHILDREN, FOREVER...

? When Noah and his family left the ark, what things were they thankful for?

? What promise did God make to Noah? What sign did He give Noah that we might see today on a rainy day?

? Think of four things that you can thank God for. (Think of your family, your friends, your church, your home, etc., when making your list.)

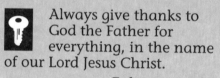
WRITE A THANK-YOU NOTE TO GOD FOR SOMETHING
YOU ARE THANKFUL FOR.

DEAR GOD,
    THANK YOU FOR _____

_____

_____

_____

_____

_____

_____

    LOVE,

Leave Everything and Go

AFTER THE PERIOD OF MOURNING...

WHAT ARE YOUR PLANS FOR THE TRIBE, ABRAHAM?

NAHOR, GOD HAS CALLED ME TO TAKE MY FAMILY—LOT'S, TOO, IF HE WISHES, AND LEAVE HARAN.

THEN the Lord said to Abram,* "Leave your **country,** your relatives and your father's family. Go to the land I will show you.
²I will make you a great nation,
    and I will bless you.
I will make you famous.
    And you will be a blessing to others.
³I will bless those who bless you.
    I will place a curse on
those who harm you.
    And all the
    people on
    earth will
    be blessed
    through you."

LEAVE? WHERE ARE YOU GOING?

I DON'T KNOW EXACTLY—BUT GOD PROMISED TO SHOW ME AND I HAVE FAITH THAT HE WILL LEAD ME.

⁴So Abram left Haran as the Lord had told him. And Lot went with him. At this time Abram was 75 years old. ⁵Abram took his wife Sarai, his nephew Lot and everything they owned. They took all the servants they had gotten in Haran. They set out from Haran, planning to go to the land of Canaan. In time they arrived there.

⁶Abram traveled through that land. He went as far as the great tree of Moreh at Shechem. The Canaanites were living in the land at that time. ⁷The Lord appeared to Abram. The Lord said, "I will give this land to your descendants." So Abram built an altar there to the Lord, who had appeared to him.   *From Genesis 12*

Morell

* *Later God changed Abram's name to Abraham.*

I TELL YOU ABRAHAM IS CRAZY. GOING SOMEPLACE...BUT HE DOESN'T KNOW WHERE!

? God asked Abraham to leave his home, his relatives, all that was familiar to him. How do you think Abraham felt about making a move like that?

? Did God promise Abraham any good rewards for taking such a big step? What were they?

? As we grow older we have to face new experiences. Sometimes that's scary. Think of something you have done that seemed scary at first, but once you did it, you felt good about yourself. (Some examples could be: learning to ride your bike, diving off the diving board, being up to bat for the first time, or moving to a new school.)

Trust the Lord with all your heart. Don't depend on your own understanding. Remember the Lord in everything you do. And he will give you success.

Proverbs 3:5, 6

MAKE A LIST OF THINGS YOU WOULD LIKE TO DO
THAT YOU'VE NEVER DONE BEFORE. HERE ARE SOME
EXAMPLES TO GET YOU STARTED: WRITE TO
SOMEONE IN A FOREIGN COUNTRY, LEARN TO PLAY A
MUSICAL INSTRUMENT, MAKE FRIENDS WITH
SOMEONE NEW AT SCHOOL, MAKE SOMETHING
OUT OF WOOD, TAKE UP A NEW SPORT.
NOW MAKE YOUR OWN LIST.
ASK THE LORD TO HELP YOU DO
ONE OF THE THINGS ON YOUR LIST
THIS NEXT YEAR. THEN BELIEVE
THAT HE WILL HELP YOU DO
IT. (YOU MIGHT BE
SURPRISED WHEN HE
ANSWERS YOUR
PRAYER!)

1

2

3

4

5

6

Thank You, God, for
always being there
to help me through the
new experiences in my life.
Help me to have the faith
to trust You more each day.
Amen.

27

A Bride for Isaac

WHEN ABRAHAM WAS OLD, HE CALLED HIS
SERVANT TO HIS SIDE. HE MADE THE
SERVANT VOW THAT HE WOULD GO TO THE
COUNTRY OF ABRAHAM'S RELATIVES TO FIND
A WIFE FOR HIS SON ISAAC. THE SERVANT
TRAVELED TO THE LAND OF ABRAHAM'S
FATHER AND THERE BY A WELL HE
PRAYED TO THE LORD. . . .

ABRAHAM'S SERVANT REACHES HARAN IN THE EVENING.
HE RESTS BY THE TOWN'S WELL AND SEES YOUNG WOMEN
OF THE CITY COMING TO GET WATER.

O GOD, GIVE ME A SIGN! LET
THE ONE WHO GIVES WATER
TO ME AND MY CAMELS
BE ISAAC'S BRIDE!

"LORD, you are the God of my master Abraham.

Allow me to find a wife for his son today. . . . 13Here I am, standing by the spring of water. The girls from the city are coming out to get water. 14I will say to one of the girls, 'Please put your jar down so I can drink.' Then let her say, 'Drink, and I will also give water to your camels.' If that happens, I will know she is the right one for your servant Isaac. And I will know that you have shown kindness to my master."

15Before the servant had finished praying, Rebekah came out of the city. . . . Rebekah was carrying her water jar on her shoulder. 16She was very pretty. She was a virgin; she had never had sexual relations with a man. She went down to the spring and filled her jar. Then she came back up. 17The servant ran to her and said, "Please give me a little water from your jar."

18Rebekah said, "Drink, sir." She quickly lowered the jar from her shoulder and gave him a drink. 19After he finished drinking, Rebekah said, "I will also pour some water for your camels." 20So she quickly poured all the water from her jar into the drinking trough for the camels. Then she kept running to the well until she had given all the camels enough to drink. . . .

26The servant bowed and worshiped the Lord.

From Genesis 24

I'LL BE GLAD TO—AND I'LL DRAW WATER FOR YOUR CAMELS, TOO.

SHE IS THE ONE!

? Did Rebekah know that if she watered the servant's camels, she would someday marry Isaac? How do you know?

? Besides giving the servant a drink, how did Rebekah show him kindness?

? We show kindness when we do nice things for people without expecting a reward or pay in return. Can you think of a time this past week when you were kind to someone or someone was kind to you? What happened?

Don't ever stop being kind and truthful. Let kindness and truth show in all you do.
Proverbs 3:3

Dear God, thank You for showing me by Your example how to be kind to others. Remind me to be kind to others each day. Amen.

More!

MAKE A LIST OF THINGS THAT YOU COULD DO THIS WEEK TO SHOW KINDNESS TO OTHERS. (DON'T FORGET TO LIST THINGS THAT YOU COULD DO FOR MOM OR DAD, YOUR TEACHER, OR AN ELDERLY PERSON WHO LIVES ON YOUR BLOCK.)

I CAN BE KIND THIS WEEK BY:

_____

_____

_____

_____

_____

GOD HAS SURPRISES IN STORE FOR YOU WHEN YOU SHOW KINDNESS TO OTHERS.

Reverence

An Expensive Pot of Soup

WHICH ONE WILL RULE OUR TRIBE AFTER ISAAC?

ESAU—IT IS HIS BIRTHRIGHT BECAUSE HE WAS BORN FIRST.

ONE day Jacob was boiling a pot of vegetable soup. Esau came in from hunting in the fields. He was weak from hunger.

³⁰So Esau said to Jacob, "Let me eat some of that red soup. I am weak with hunger." (That is why people call him Edom.)

³¹But Jacob said, "You must sell me your rights as the firstborn son."

³²Esau said, "I am almost dead from hunger. If I die, all of my father's wealth will not help me."

³³But Jacob said, "First, promise me that you will give it to me." So Esau made a promise to Jacob. In this way he sold his part of their father's wealth to Jacob.

³⁴Then Jacob gave Esau bread and vegetable soup. Esau ate and drank and then left. So Esau showed how little he cared about his rights as the firstborn son.

From Genesis 25

? What was Esau's biggest problem when he came home from hunting?

? The firstborn son received twice the inheritance of any family member (Deut. 21:17), and he received special treatment from his father. Someday the son would become leader of the family. Do you think that Esau thought about what he'd be losing when he traded his inheritance for a bowl of soup?

? Esau didn't show reverence or respect for what was really important in his life. Sometimes we are like that when we don't show reverence for God and His house. We don't act as though the things of God are important to us. Name some ways that we don't show reverence to God. (Some examples are: talking while the pastor is preaching, passing notes in church, not picking up litter left in the pew, etc.)

More!▐▐▐➡

31

"Remember my Sabbaths, and respect my Holy Place. I am the Lord."
Leviticus 26:2

Dear God, thank You for loving me and giving me a church to go to. Help me always to reverence You and Your house. Amen

ONE THING I WILL DO THIS WEEK TO SHOW REVERENCE TO GOD IS:

1

The Secret Is Out

AS A BOY, JOSEPH WAS SOLD INTO SLAVERY BY HIS TEN BROTHERS. BUT GOD BLESSED JOSEPH AND HE BECAME THE GOVERNOR OF EGYPT. YEARS LATER WHEN FAMINE STRUCK THE LAND, HIS BROTHERS WENT TO EGYPT TO BUY GRAIN FROM JOSEPH. THEY DID NOT RECOGNIZE THE GOVERNOR AS BEING THEIR BROTHER JOSEPH. HE TESTS HIS BROTHERS TO SEE IF THEY HAVE CHANGED. AS A FINAL TEST, HE HAS HIS CUP PUT IN HIS YOUNGEST BROTHER'S GRAIN SACK.

YOUR MASTER'S CUP? WE ARE INNOCENT! SEARCH US IF YOU WILL.

IF THE CUP IS FOUND, THE MAN IN WHOSE SACK IT IS HIDDEN SHALL BECOME MY MASTER'S SLAVE!

ONE BY ONE THE SACKS ARE SEARCHED... AT LAST THE OFFICER OPENS BENJAMIN'S...

THE CUP!

THE ONE IN WHOSE BAG THE CUP WAS FOUND SHALL BE MY SERVANT— THE REST OF YOU MAY RETURN TO YOUR FATHER.

IF BENJAMIN DOES NOT RETURN HOME, OUR FATHER WILL DIE OF GRIEF. LET ME BE YOUR SLAVE INSTEAD OF BENJAMIN.

THEY LISTENED IN SHOCK AS HE SPOKE THESE WORDS.

"**I AM** Joseph. Is my father still alive?" But the brothers could not answer him, because they were very afraid of him.

⁴So Joseph said to them, "Come close to me." So the brothers came close to him. And he said to them, "I am your brother Joseph. You sold me as a slave to go to Egypt. ⁵Now don't be worried. Don't be angry with yourselves

because you sold me here. God sent me here ahead of you to save people's lives. ⁶No food has grown on the land for two years now. And there will be five more years without planting or harvest. ⁷So God sent me here ahead of you. This was to make sure you have some descendants left on earth. And it was to keep you alive in an amazing way. ⁸So it was not you who sent me here, but God. God has made me the highest officer of the king of Egypt. I am in charge of his palace. I am the master of all the land of Egypt."

From Genesis 45

? If you were Joseph, what thoughts would have gone through your mind regarding your brothers during the long years between being sold and facing them as a governor? Did Joseph have the power to get revenge in the end?

? Why do you think it's so hard for us to forgive someone who has done something to hurt us?

? God's Word tells us that we are forgiven as we forgive others. How can we practice forgiving others?

I BELIEVE IT WAS GOD'S WILL THAT I CAME TO EGYPT TO SAVE YOUR LIVES— AND THE LIVES OF OTHERS— IN THIS FAMINE.

> If you forgive others for the things they do wrong, then your Father in heaven will also forgive you for the things you do wrong.
>
> Matthew 6:14

Thank You, God, for the many times You have forgiven me for things I've done wrong. Help me to be forgiving of others who hurt me with their words and actions. I want to be more like You. Amen.

THINK OF SOMETHING THAT HAPPENED THIS PAST WEEK THAT YOU NEED TO ASK FORGIVENESS FOR. PERHAPS YOU SAID OR DID SOMETHING TO HURT SOMEONE'S FEELINGS, OR YOU TOLD YOUR PARENTS SOMETHING THAT WASN'T TRUE. IN YOUR OWN WORDS, WRITE OUT HOW YOU WOULD ASK FOR FORGIVENESS FROM THAT PERSON. (BE SURE TO SAY SPECIFICALLY WHAT IT IS THAT YOU'VE DONE THAT NEEDS FORGIVE-NESS.) THEN ASK GOD TO HELP YOU GO TO THAT PERSON AND SAY THE WORDS YOU'VE WRITTEN DOWN.

Miriam and the Boat Basket

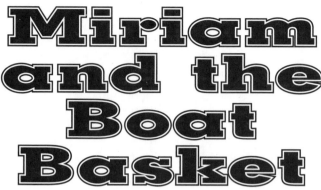

NEXT DAY THE MOTHER SETS AB?
PREPARING A LITTLE BASKET.

KEEP WATCH, MIRIAM, I'M ALMOST FINISHED.

BUT **after three months, she was not able to hide the baby any longer.** So she got a basket made of reeds and covered it with tar so that it would float. She put the baby in the basket. Then she put the basket among the tall grass at the edge of the Nile River. ⁴The baby's sister stood a short distance away. She wanted to see what would happen to him.

LOOK—WHAT A STRANGE LITTLE BASKET! I WONDER WHAT'S INSIDE IT?

⁵Then the daughter of the king of Egypt came to the river. She was going to take a bath. Her servant girls were walking beside the river. She saw the basket in the tall grass. So she sent her slave girl to get it. ⁶The king's daughter opened the basket and saw the baby boy. He was crying, and she felt sorry for him. She said, "This is one of the Hebrew babies."

AT THIS POINT MIRIAM STEPS FORTH.

SHALL I FIND A HEBREW NURSE FOR THE BABY?

YES—BRING HER TO ME AS SOON AS YOU CAN.

⁷Then the baby's sister asked the king's daughter, "Would you like me to find a Hebrew woman to nurse the baby for you?"

⁸The king's daughter said, "Yes, please." So the girl went and got the baby's own mother.

⁹The king's daughter said to the woman, "Take this baby and nurse him for me. I will pay you." So the woman took her baby and nursed him. ¹⁰After the child had grown older, the woman took him to the king's daughter. She adopted the baby as her own son. The king's daughter named him Moses, because she had pulled him out of the water.

From Exodus 2

? How did Miriam help both the princess and her mother?

? What might have happened to the baby if Miriam hadn't taken the initiative to speak up?

? Miriam saw an opportunity to take action and she did it quickly. Looking at the situation calmly, getting an idea for a solution, and then carrying it through was the key to Miriam saving her brother's life. Think about a problem your class is having at school (examples: the kid next to you won't stop talking, kids taking too long to come in from recess, kids getting into other kids' desks, etc.). What is one idea that you could contribute to help resolve the problem? (Share your idea with your teacher.)

 Lord, teach me your ways. Guide me to do what is right. . . .
Psalm 27:11

Lord, thank You for the abilities You have given me. Help me to think of ways to be more helpful when answers to problems are needed. Amen.

THINK OF ONE
PROBLEM YOU ARE
HAVING WITH A FAMILY
MEMBER AT HOME.
THINK OF ONE WAY
THAT YOU COULD
RESOLVE THE
PROBLEM. DRAW A
PICTURE OF YOUR IDEA.

SHARE YOUR IDEA WITH
MOM OR DAD AND SEE
IF YOU CAN ALL WORK
TOGETHER TO RESOLVE
THE PROBLEM.

That Bush Is on Fire!

HERE AM I!

ONE day Moses was taking care of Jethro's sheep. Jethro was the priest of Midian and also Moses' father-in-law. Moses led the sheep to the west side of the desert. He came to Sinai, the mountain of God. ²There the angel of the Lord appeared to Moses in flames of fire coming out of a bush. Moses saw that the bush was on fire, but it was not burning up. ³So Moses said, "I will go closer to this strange thing. How can a bush continue burning without burning up?"

⁴The Lord saw Moses was coming to look at the bush. So God called to him from the bush, "Moses, Moses!"

And Moses said, "Here I am."

⁵Then God said, "Do not come any closer. Take off your sandals. You are standing on holy ground. ⁶I am the God of your ancestors. I am the God of Abraham, the God of Isaac and the God of Jacob." Moses covered his face because he was afraid to look at God. ⁹I have heard the cries of the people of Israel. I have seen the way the Egyptians have made life hard for them. ¹⁰So now I am sending you to the king of Egypt. Go! Bring my people, the Israelites, out of Egypt!"

¹¹But Moses said to God, "I am not a great man! Why should I be the one to go to the king and lead the Israelites out of Egypt?"

¹²God said, "I will be with you. This will be the proof that I am sending you: You will lead the people out of Egypt. Then all of you will worship me on this mountain."

From Exodus 3

More▶

? What was unusual about the bush that Moses saw?

? Someone or something that is set apart—being consecrated or dedicated to God—is referred to as "holy" in the Bible. What did God call the place where Moses was standing?

? God called Moses to be set apart to do a special job. What was that job?

? We as Christians are set apart or chosen by God to do special things for Him. We are not usually asked to go before a king or president to bring deliverance to a nation, but there are many smaller ways that we can show Jesus' love to those around us. (Some examples are: doing something nice for a neighbor or your mom and dad!, writing a note to cheer someone up, baking cookies for a student away at school, etc.) What is one thing that you could do this week?

But you are chosen people. . . .You are a holy nation. You are a nation that belongs to God alone. God chose you to tell about the wonderful things he has done.

I Peter 2:9

Thank You, God, for making me special to You. Help me to think of ways to share Your love with others.
Amen.

PRETEND THAT YOU ARE STARTING A NEW CLUB--THE CHOSEN KIDS' CLUB (CKC). MAKE A LIST OF FRIENDS WHO COULD BELONG TO THE CLUB, AND BESIDE EACH NAME WRITE ONE THING THAT PERSON COULD DO TO SHARE JESUS' LOVE WITH SOMEONE ELSE.

1 _____

2 _____

3 _____

4 _____

5 _____

TALK TO YOUR FRIENDS AND SEE IF THEY WOULD LIKE TO START A CKC. THERE ARE LOTS OF WAYS THAT KIDS CAN BE INVOLVED IN SHARING GOD'S LOVE!

Songs of Joy

THE ISRAELITES FACED THE RED SEA. THE EGYPTIAN ARMY CHARGED THEM FROM BEHIND. WHAT COULD THE ISRAELITES DO? . . . MOSES HELD OUT HIS HAND OVER THE SEA AND THE LORD SPLIT THE SEA.

BUT **Moses answered, "Don't be afraid!** Stand still and see the Lord save you today. You will never see these Egyptians again after today.

21Moses held his hand over the sea. All that night the Lord drove back the sea with a strong east wind. And so he made the sea become dry ground. The water was split. 22And the Israelites went through the sea on dry land. A wall of water was on both sides. 23Then all the king's horses, chariots and chariot drivers followed them into the sea. . . . 27So Moses raised his hand over the sea. And at dawn the water became deep again. . . . 28All the king's army . . . was covered. Not one of them survived. . . .

30So that day the Lord saved the Israelites from the Egyptians. . . .31When the people of Israel saw the great power that the Lord had used against the Egyptians, they feared the Lord. And they trusted the Lord and his servant Moses.

Chapter 15Then Aaron's sister Miriam, who was a prophetess, took a tambourine in her hand. All the women followed her, playing tambourines and dancing. 21Miriam told them:

"Sing to the Lord
because he is worthy of great honor.
He has thrown the horse and its rider
into the sea."

From Exodus 14, 15

AWED BY THE SIGHT, THE HEBREWS RUSH JOYFULLY ACROSS THE PATH IN THE SEA.

IN TERROR THEY TRY TO TURN BACK... BUT THE WIND DIES, AND THE WATERS RETURN. ALL OF PHARAOH'S MEN ARE CAUGHT IN THE RUSHING SEA.

? Did the Israelites have reason to rejoice? Why?

? The Israelites were glad that God kept them from being captured, but what else did they learn about God's ability to take care of them?

? It's easy to be happy when special things happen in our lives. But we can experience a deeper joy in our hearts when we realize that no matter what's happening—good or bad—God is there loving us, taking care of us. List two things that have happened in your life in the last month that maybe weren't so great. How did God help you through those times?

Don't be sad. The joy of the Lord will make you strong.

Nehemiah 8:10b

Thanks, God, for always being there when I need You–in good times and bad. Help me to feel Your joy and strength today. Amen.

WHEN I FEEL THE JOY OF THE LORD IN MY HEART, MY FACE LOOKS LIKE THIS: (DRAW A PICTURE OF YOUR FACE.)

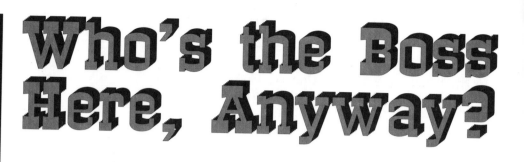

Who's the Boss Here, Anyway?

MIRIAM **and Aaron began to talk against Moses,** who had married a Cushite. ²They said to themselves, "Is Moses the only one the Lord speaks through? Doesn't he speak through us?" And the Lord heard this.

³(Now Moses was very humble. He was the least proud person on earth.)

⁴So the Lord suddenly spoke to Moses, Aaron and Miriam. He said, "All three of you come to the Meeting Tent now." So they went. ⁵The Lord came down in a pillar of cloud. He stood at the entrance to the Tent. He called to Aaron and Miriam, and they both came near. ⁶He said, "Listen to my words:

THEN GOD SPEAKS FROM A CLOUD, AND TELLS THEM THAT HE HAS CHOSEN MOSES TO LEAD THE PEOPLE OF ISRAEL. WHEN THE CLOUD DISAPPEARS, MIRIAM AND AARON GET THE SHOCK OF THEIR LIVES.

¹⁰ Then Aaron turned toward Miriam. She was as white as snow. She had a harmful skin disease. ¹¹Aaron said to Moses, "Please, my master, forgive us for our foolish sin. . . .

¹³So Moses cried out to the Lord, "God, please heal her!"

From Numbers 12

? How did God tell Miriam and Aaron who was really in charge?

? What resulted when they rebelled against Moses? What did they do to make things right with Moses?

? Sometimes it's easy to criticize the people who are in charge — our parents, teachers, youth leaders. We don't see all the different sides to every decision they have to make. Rather than rebel against that person, what is a better way to handle the situation?

Let us examine and look at what we have done. Then let us return to the Lord.
Lamentations 3:40

God, sometimes I rebel against those who You've put over me. Help me to repent and ask forgiveness when I don't act in a way that is pleasing to You. Amen.

More⟶

TAKE A MINUTE TO THINK ABOUT A TIME WHEN YOU REBELLED AGAINST SOMEONE WHO WAS IN CHARGE. HOW DID YOU HANDLE THE SITUATION? IF YOU FEEL THAT YOU SHOULD ASK FORGIVENESS FOR YOUR ACTIONS, WRITE DOWN TWO SENTENCES THAT YOU COULD TELL THAT PERSON.

_____

_____

_____

_____

_____

_____

_____

_____

_____

_____

_____

ASK GOD TO HELP YOU FIND AN OPPORTUNITY TO TELL HIM OR HER YOUR WORDS IN PERSON.

Spies in the Land

THEY **came back to Moses and Aaron** and all the Israelites at Kadesh. . . . "We went to the land where you sent us. It is a land where much food grows! Here is some of its fruit. 28But the people who live there are strong. Their cities are walled and large."

30Then Caleb told the people near Moses to be quiet. Caleb said, "We should go up and take the land for ourselves. We can do it."

31But the men who had gone with him said, "We can't attack those people. They are stronger than

we are." 32And those men gave the Israelites a bad report about the land they explored. They said, "The land would eat us up. All the people we saw are very tall . . . We felt like grasshoppers. And we looked like grasshoppers to them."

Chapter 14That night all the people in the camp began crying loudly . . . "We should

have died in Egypt. Or we should have died in the desert. 3Why is the Lord bringing us to this land? We will be killed with swords. Our wives and children will be taken away. We would be better off going back to Egypt."

5Then Moses and Aaron bowed facedown in front of all the Israelites gathered there. . . . They tore their clothes. 7They said to all of the Israelites, "The land we went to explore is very good. 8If the Lord is pleased with us, he will lead us into that land. He will give us that land where much food grows. 9Don't turn against the Lord! Don't be afraid of the people in that land! We will chew them up. They have no protection, but we have the Lord. So don't be afraid of them."

From Numbers 13, 14

? What were the good things about the new land? . . . the bad things?

? Why was it easier to believe the bad report? Do you think it made a difference that more spies gave a bad report than the few who gave a good report?

? The spies told Moses that they felt like grasshoppers next to the men in Canaan. The devil tries to make us feel like the size of grasshoppers when we look at things we are afraid of (examples: being afraid of the dark, afraid to meet new people, afraid of being lonely or rejected). We feel like we will never get over our fear. But if we put our trust in God, He will help us conquer our fears. Think of one fear that you would like God to help you overcome.

 If you trust the Lord, you will be safe.

Proverbs 29:25

Lord, thank You for caring about me. Help me to trust that You will take care of the "grasshoppers" in my life. Amen.

SOMETIMES IT'S EASIER TO BELIEVE A BAD REPORT AND NOT TRY SOMETHING NEW THAN TO TRUST GOD TO HELP YOU DO IT. THINK OF SOMETHING YOU WOULD LIKE TO DO BUT HAVE BEEN AFRAID TO TRY (EXAMPLES: TAKE SWIMMING LESSONS OR JOIN LITTLE LEAGUE). WRITE ONE GOOD THING AND ONE BAD THING THAT YOU WILL KNOW IF YOU DO THIS EXAMPLE:

SOMETHING NEW: TAKE SWIMMING LESSONS
SOMETHING GOOD: I WILL LEARN TO SWIM.
SOMETHING BAD: I WILL HAVE TO GO TO A LESSON EVERY MORNING FOR TWO WEEKS.

YOUR LIST:

SOMETHING NEW:

SOMETHING GOOD:

SOMETHING BAD:

Rahab Takes a Chance

When Joshua's two spies enter Jericho they avoid the public inn and seek lodging in the house of a woman named Rahab.

We are strangers in your city—may we have a room here for the night?

Yes—

The king's soldier is suspicious of these men! I'll find out what brings them here.

When the king found out Joshua's men were in town. He sent his men to go take them prisoner.

I hear footsteps—quick—I'll hide you on the roof.

More⟩

HIDE OUT IN THE MOUNTAINS FOR THREE DAYS—AFTER THAT IT WILL BE SAFE FOR YOU TO CROSS THE RIVER TO YOUR OWN CAMP.

WHEN THE ATTACK COMES, KEEP YOUR FAMILY IN THE HOUSE ...AND TIE THIS RED ROPE IN YOUR WINDOW SO OUR MEN WILL KNOW WHERE YOU LIVE!

RAHAB HID THE SCOUTS ON THE ROOF OF HER HOUSE. IN RETURN FOR PROTECTING THEM, RAHAB SAID . . .

"**So** now, make me a promise before the **Lord.** Promise that you will show kindness to my family just as I showed you kindness. Give me some proof that you will do this. 13Promise me you will allow my family to live. Save my father, mother, brothers, sisters and all of their families from death."

14The men agreed. They said, "We will trade our lives for your lives. Don't tell anyone what we are doing. When the Lord gives us our land, we will be kind to you. You may trust us."

15The house Rahab lived in was built on the city wall. So she used a rope to let the men down through a window.

18"You are using a red rope to help us escape. When we return to this land, you must tie it in the window through which you let us down. Bring your father, mother, brothers and all your family into your house. 19We can keep everyone safe who stays in this house. If anyone in your house is hurt, we will be responsible. If anyone goes out of your house and is killed, it is his own fault. We cannot be responsible for him."

Chapter 6Joshua saved Rahab the prostitute, her family and all who were with her. He let them live. This was because Rahab had helped the men he had sent to spy out Jericho. Rahab still lives among the Israelites today.

50

From Joshua 2, 6

? How did Rahab help the two men? What promise did the men give Rahab?

? Everything goes more smoothly when all cooperate to get the work done. In this case, the scouts and Rahab worked together to get necessary information back to the Israelite leader, Joshua. What would have happened if Rahab turned the scouts over to the king's men?

? Working together with a friend makes the job seem fun and takes less time. Ask a friend to help you work on a job around your house (examples: putting away the clean dishes, raking leaves, cleaning the garage, etc.). Write down the time it took for the two of you to do the job. Then go to your friend's house and help him or her with a similar job. Again, write the time down. Which job took the least amount of working-together time?

*Dear God,
thank You for giving
me friends so that we can
work together to do things that
honor You. Help me always to be a
willing worker. Amen.*

"I tell you that if two of you on earth agree about something, then you can pray for it. And the thing you ask for will be done for you by my Father in heaven."

Matthew 18:19

YOU CAN COOPERATE WITH A FRIEND IN DOING FUN THINGS, TOO. TOGETHER MAKE A CARD OR DRAW A PICTURE TO SEND SOMEONE IN YOUR CHURCH WHO HAS BEEN SICK. WHEN YOU'RE FINISHED WITH YOUR PROJECT, MAKE A LARGE ICE-CREAM SUNDAE OR ANOTHER TREAT THAT YOU CAN SPLIT. DRAW A PICTURE OF YOU AND YOUR FRIEND COOPERATING TOGETHER IN EATING!

NOW the people of Jericho were afraid because the Israelites were near. So they closed the city gates and guarded them. No one went into the city. And no one came out.

2Then the Lord spoke to Joshua. He said, "Look, I have given you Jericho, its king and all its fighting men. 3March around the city with your army one time every day. Do this for six days. 4Have seven priests carry trumpets made from horns of male sheep. Tell them to march in front of the Holy Box. On the seventh day march around the city seven times. On that day tell the priests to blow the trumpets as they march. 5They will make one long blast on the trumpets. When you hear that sound, have all the people give a loud shout. Then the walls of the city will fall. And the people will go straight into the city."

20When the priests blew the trumpets, the people shouted. At the sound of the trumpets and the people's shout, the walls fell. And everyone ran straight into the city. So the Israelites defeated that city.

27So the Lord was with Joshua. And Joshua became famous through all the land.   *From Joshua 6*

VICTORY

God's Way

? After the first day of marching, what if Joshua would have said, "I'm tired! It's a long trip marching around Jericho. I think we'll only march one more day." What would have happened?

? Why were the instructions that God gave Joshua so unusual? (Remember: Joshua was the leader of the whole Israelite army.) Do soldiers normally fight this way?

? Following God's orders is very important to our Christian growth. If we want to be like Him, we have to do what He says in His Word. Sometimes the orders seem strange to us. For example, in Matthew 18:21, 22, how many times are we suppose to forgive someone who does something against us? How is this different from the way most people think?

JERICHO IS OURS!

Morell

Help me obey your
commands because that
makes me happy.
Psalm 119:35

*Thank You, God, for teaching me
Your ways. Help me to follow
Your directions even when they
seem strange to me. Amen.*

LET'S INVESTIGATE OTHER
THINGS GOD'S WORD
TELLS US TO DO. LOOK
UP THESE VERSES IN
YOUR BIBLE AND THEN
WRITE A SHORT
SENTENCE ABOUT HOW
YOU CAN FOLLOW GOD'S
DIRECTIONS IN YOUR LIFE.
⇨ MATTHEW 5:44--
I CAN PRAY FOR PEOPLE
WHO GO AGAINST ME.
⇨ MATTHEW 7:12--

⇨ LUKE 6:38--

ASK GOD TO HELP YOU
FOLLOW WHAT HIS WORD
TELLS US TO DO.

A Secret Hidden in a Tent

"DON'T take any of **the things that are to be destroyed** as an offering to the Lord. If you take them and bring them into our camp, then you yourselves will be destroyed. You will also bring trouble to all of Israel. ¹⁹All the silver and gold and things made from bronze and iron belong to the Lord. They must be saved for him."

Chapter 7But the people of Israel did not obey the Lord. There was a man from the tribe of Judah named Achan. . . . Achan kept some of the things that were to be given to the Lord. So the Lord became very angry at the Israelites.

From Joshua 6, 7

HO, LOOK AT THEM RUN. THEY'RE AFRAID TO FIGHT.

SO THESE ARE THE BRAVE ISRAELITES WHO TOOK JERICHO!

THAT NIGHT WHILE THE REST OF THE CAMP SLEEPS HE BURIES HIS STOLEN TREASURE.

THIS WILL HELP ME GET STARTED IN THIS NEW LAND.

LATER, WHEN THE ARMY ATTACKED THE SMALL CITY OF AI, THE SOLDIERS WERE ROUTED, AND JOSHUA WAS SHOCKED. HE ASKED THE LORD WHY, AND GOD SAID THAT IT WAS BECAUSE SOMEONE HAD DISOBEYED. More!!!➡ 55

IT IS TRUE—I SINNED AGAINST GOD AND MY PEOPLE.

NOW WE STAND RIGHT WITH GOD.

EARLY the next morning Joshua led all of Israel

before the Lord. All of the tribes stood before him. And the Lord chose the tribe of Judah. [17]So all the family groups of Judah stood before the Lord. The Lord then chose the family group of Zerah. And all the families of Zerah stood before the Lord. Then the family of Zimri was chosen. [18]And Joshua told all the men in that family to come before the Lord. The Lord chose Achan son of Carmi. . . .

[19]Then Joshua said to Achan, "My son, you should tell the truth. Confess to the Lord, the God of Israel. Tell me what you did. Don't try to hide anything from me."

But if we confess our sins, he will forgive our sins. We can trust God. He does what is right. He will make us clean from all the wrongs we have done.

I John 1:9

God, help me always to be honest with You, and ask forgiveness when I'm wrong. Amen.

? What was the command that Joshua gave the Israelites? Who was supposed to get the captured goods?

? What did Achan do with the robe, gold and silver? Did his dishonesty go unnoticed?

? God sees everything we do. When we do things that are wrong, we need to confess and tell the truth. Achan not only did not confess when he took the items, but he didn't come forward when Joshua was questioning the people. Think of something that you have not been completely honest about. What can you do to make things right with God?

WRITE A NOTE TO GOD EXPLAINING A TIME WHEN YOU WERE NOT HONEST. THEN READ THE NOTE ALOUD TO GOD, AND CLOSE BY ASKING HIM TO FORGIVE YOU.

DEAR GOD,

Ruth Finds a New Home

ONE DAY Ruth, the woman from Moab, said to Naomi, **"Let me go to the fields.** Maybe someone will be kind and let me gather the grain he leaves in his field."

Naomi said, "Go, my daughter."

³So Ruth went to the fields. She followed the workers who were cutting the grain. And she gathered the grain that they had left. It just so happened that the field belonged to Boaz. . . .

⁸Then Boaz said to Ruth, "Listen, my daughter. Stay here in my field to gather grain for yourself. Do not go to any other person's field. Continue following behind my women workers. ⁹Watch to see which fields they go to and follow them. I have warned the young men not to bother you. When you are thirsty, you may go and drink. Take water from the water jugs that the servants have filled."

¹⁰Then Ruth bowed low with her face to the ground. She said to Boaz, "I am a stranger. Why have you been so kind to notice me?"

¹¹Boaz answered her, "I know about all the help you have given to Naomi, your mother-in-law. You helped her even after your husband died. You left your father and mother and your own country. You came to this nation where you did not know anyone. ¹²The Lord will reward you for all you have done. You will be paid in full by the Lord, the God of Israel. You have come to him as a little bird finds shelter under the wings of its mother."

From Ruth 2

HER NAME IS RUTH—SHE IS THE MOABITE WOMAN WHO TAKES CARE OF HER MOTHER-IN-LAW, NAOMI.

HOW BEAUTIFUL SHE IS!

? What did Ruth do to help Naomi?

? What special thing did Boaz do for Ruth when she gathered grain in his field?

? Ruth showed loyalty by leaving her homeland to travel with and care for Naomi. No matter what happened, Ruth would not leave Naomi. A true friend shows loyalty by sticking close by you no matter what happens. Think about three qualities you would like to have in a friend (example: a friend should listen when you feel like talking about your problems, or a friend is someone you can share any secret with).

DROP SOME GRAIN ON PURPOSE FOR HER TO PICK UP. AND SEE THAT NO HARM COMES TO HER!

HAVE NO FEAR, BOAZ. SHE WILL BE SAFE—AND SHE WILL FIND ALL THE GRAIN SHE NEEDS.

A person who tries to live right and be loyal finds life, success and honor.

Proverbs 21:21

God, thank You for giving me family and friends who care about me. Help me to show loyalty to them by saying kind things to encourage them. Amen.

WE SHOW LOYALTY TO OUR FAMILY BY DEFENDING IT WHEN OTHERS SAY HURTFUL WORDS AGAINST IT. YOU CAN BUILD STRONG LOYALTY BY SAYING POSITIVE THINGS ABOUT ONE ANOTHER TO MAKE EACH MEMBER FEEL IMPORTANT TO THE FAMILY. WRITE ONE POSITIVE THING ABOUT EACH MEMBER OF YOUR FAMILY.

ON SEPARATE PIECES OF PAPER, WRITE THE POSITIVE COMMENTS. THEN HIDE EACH NOTE UNDER THE PILLOW OF THE PERSON FOR WHOM THE COMMENT WAS INTENDED.

59

A Promise for Hannah

After they had eaten their meal in Shiloh, Hannah got up. Now Eli the priest was sitting on a chair near the entrance to the Lord's Holy Tent. 10Hannah was very sad. She cried much and prayed to the Lord. 11She made a promise. She said, "Lord of heaven's armies, see how bad I feel. Remember me! Don't forget me. If you will give me a son, I will give him back to you all his life. And no one will ever use a razor to cut his hair."

12While Hannah kept praying, Eli watched her mouth. 13She was praying in her heart. Her lips moved, but her voice was not heard. So Eli thought she was drunk. 14He said to her, "Stop getting drunk! Throw away your wine!"

15Hannah answered, "No, master, I have not drunk any wine or beer. I am a woman who is deeply troubled. I was telling the Lord about all my problems. 16Don't think of me as an evil woman. I have been praying because of my many troubles and much sadness."

17Eli answered, "Go in peace. May the God of Israel give you what you asked of him."

18Hannah said, "I want to be pleasing to you always." Then she left and ate something. She was not sad anymore.

From I Samuel 1

ANGRILY HE ACCUSES HER...

NO! NO! I AM NOT DRUNK, I AM UNHAPPY; AND IN MY SORROW I HAVE POURED OUT MY HEART TO GOD, ASKING HIM TO HELP ME.

? How did Hannah let God know what she wanted?

? What promise did Eli give Hannah?

? Sometimes there are situations in our lives that seem impossible. But God is able to help us with any problem. All we have to do is to pray and ask God for His help. What is one thing you would like God to work out in your life?

Remain in me and follow my teachings. If you do this, then you can ask for anything you want, and it will be given to you.

John 15:7

Lord, help me to pray to You for the things I need. Thank You for always being there to answer. Amen.

Morell➡

WHEN PEOPLE SPEAK THEIR NEEDS, WE CALL THEM PRAYER REQUESTS. A REQUEST IS SOMETHING WE ARE ASKING GOD TO TAKE CARE OF. WRITE SEVERAL PRAYER REQUESTS ON THE LINES BELOW.

MY REQUESTS ARE:

THANK YOU, GOD, FOR ANSWERING PRAYERS.

MY NAME:

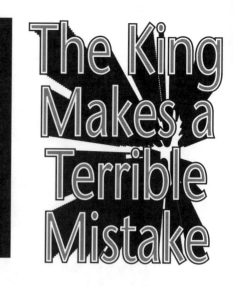

Wisdom

The King Makes a Terrible Mistake

SAUL **waited seven days,** because Samuel had said he would meet him then. But Samuel did not come to Gilgal. And the soldiers began to leave.

⁹So Saul said, "Bring me the whole burnt offering and the fellowship offerings." Then Saul offered the whole burnt offering. ¹⁰Just as he finished, Samuel arrived. Saul went to meet him.

¹¹Samuel asked, "What have you done?"

Saul answered, "I saw the soldiers leaving me, and you were not here. The Philistines were gathering at Micmash. ¹²Then I thought, 'The Philistines will come against me at Gilgal. And I haven't asked for the Lord's approval.' So I forced myself to offer the whole burnt offering."

¹³Samuel said, "You acted foolishly! You haven't obeyed God's command. If you had obeyed him, God would make your kingdom continue in Israel forever. ¹⁴But now your kingdom will not continue. The Lord has looked for the kind of man he wants. The Lord has appointed him to become ruler of his people. He is doing this because you haven't obeyed his command."

From I Samuel 13

TAKE THIRTY THOUSAND CHARIOTS, SIX THOUSAND HORSEMEN AND ALL OUR INFANTRY—SET UP A CAMP AT MICHMASH. FROM THERE WE CAN SEND OUT RAIDING PARTIES THAT WILL DRAW SAUL FROM HIS STRONGHOLD AT GILGAL.

THE PHILISTINES OUTNUMBER US BY THOUSANDS. I'M HIDING OUT UNTIL THIS IS OVER.

THERE'S A PIT DOWN THE VALLEY— I'LL HIDE THERE.

THE MEN ARE LOSING THEIR NERVE. WE CAN'T WAIT MUCH LONGER FOR SAMUEL TO COME AND OFFER THE SACRIFICE TO GOD.

YOU'RE RIGHT. WE'LL WAIT NO LONGER. I'LL MAKE THE OFFERING!

? Saul took things into his own hands and didn't wait for Samuel. What did Saul do that angered Samuel?

? What did Samuel tell Saul?

? When God doesn't answer as fast as we'd like Him to, sometimes we make bad choices to work things out ourselves. Think of a time when you made a bad choice to accomplish a goal (examples: copied someone else's homework, covered up for a friend's wrongdoing, joined others in making fun of someone even though you really didn't want to do it). How did you feel about making the bad choice?

More

Dear God, thank You for Your Word that teaches us how to live. Help me to make wise choices as I'm learning to be like You. Amen.

"Now, my children, listen to me. Those who follow my ways are happy. Listen to my teaching, and you will be wise. Do not ignore it."

Proverbs 8:32, 33

LET'S DO A QUICK CHECK. THE NEXT TIME YOU ARE FACED WITH A DIFFICULT DECISION, ASK YOURSELF THESE QUESTIONS.
WILL MY ACTIONS BE:
  ❑ GOOD FOR ME?
  ❑ GOOD FOR THE OTHER PERSON INVOLVED?
  ❑ PLEASING TO GOD?
ASKING THESE QUESTIONS WILL HELP YOU TO ACT WISELY.

WRITE A PROMISE TELLING GOD YOU WILL THINK BEFORE YOU ACT THE NEXT TIME A DIFFICULT DECISION COMES UP.

_____

_____

_____

_____

_____

A Giant? No Problem!

SEND OUT A MAN WHO DARES TO FIGHT ME. IF HE KILLS ME, THE PHILISTINES WILL BE YOUR SERVANTS, BUT IF I KILL HIM, YOU WILL BE OUR SERVANTS.

EVERY DAY THAT GIANT DEFIES US. I HAVE OFFERED A HANDSOME REWARD —EVEN MY DAUGHTER IN MARRIAGE— BUT NOT ONE SOLDIER IN MY WHOLE ARMY WILL ACCEPT THE CHALLENGE.

A SHEPHERD BOY! YOU CAN'T FIGHT A GIANT!

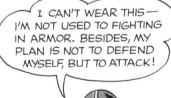

I CAN'T WEAR THIS— I'M NOT USED TO FIGHTING IN ARMOR. BESIDES, MY PLAN IS NOT TO DEFEND MYSELF, BUT TO ATTACK!

Morell▆▆▆➤

HE **took his stick in his hand.** And he chose five smooth stones from a stream. He put them in his pouch and held his sling in his hand. Then he went to meet Goliath.

⁴¹At the same time, the Philistine was coming closer to David. The man who held his shield walked in front of him. ⁴²Goliath looked at David. He saw that David was only a boy, tanned and handsome. He looked down at David with disgust. ⁴³He said, "Do you think I am a dog, that you come at me with a stick?" He used his gods' names to curse David. ⁴⁴He said to David, "Come here. I'll feed your body to the birds of the air and the wild animals!"

⁴⁵But David said to him, "You come to me using a sword, a large spear and a small spear. But I come to you in the name of the Lord of heaven's armies. . . . You have spoken out against him. ⁴⁶Today the Lord will give you to me. I'll kill you, and I'll cut off your head. . . . Then all the world will know there is a God in Israel! ⁴⁷Everyone gathered here

From I Samuel 17

will know the Lord does not need swords or spears to save people. The battle belongs to him! And he will help us defeat all of you."

⁴⁸As Goliath came near to attack him, David ran quickly to meet him. ⁴⁹He took a stone from his pouch. He put it into his sling and slung it. The stone hit the Philistine on his forehead and sank into it. Goliath fell facedown on the ground.

⁵⁰So David defeated the Philistine with only a sling and a stone! He hit him and killed him. He did not even have a sword in his hand. ⁵¹David ran and stood beside the Philistine. He took Goliath's sword out of its holder and killed him. Then he cut off Goliath's head.

When the Philistines saw that their champion was dead, they turned and ran.

? Why wasn't Goliath afraid of David? Why wasn't David afraid of Goliath?

? What were the differences between David and Goliath?

? David's purpose was clear—anyone who spoke against the Lord God of Israel must be brought down. David never wavered; he never doubted God's ability to help him complete the task. What he knew of God strengthened him for the job.

? Take a watch with a second hand. For one minute, say as many things that you know about God as you can (examples: God answers prayer, He loves people, He died on the cross so that we can be saved, etc.).

Lord, teach me what you want me to do. And I will live by your truth.

Psalm 86:11

Lord, help me purpose in my heart to serve You with my thoughts, my words, my actions. Daily give me strength to do what is right according to Your Word. Amen.

GOLIATH'S DEAD!

DRAW FIVE STONES. ON EACH STONE, WRITE ONE WAY THAT GOD HELPS YOU TO BECOME STRONG IN HIM. SOME EXAMPLES ARE: GOD ANSWERS MY PRAYERS, GOD GIVES ME STRENGTH, GOD GIVES ME HIS WORD, ETC.

WHEN YOU FEEL DISCOURAGED, TURN TO THIS PAGE AND READ ALOUD THESE FIVE THINGS. BY DOING THIS, GOD WILL STRENGTHEN AND HELP YOU.

Jonathan Saves a Friend's Life

THANK YOU, JONATHAN. GOD IS MY WITNESS THAT I WILL BE YOUR FRIEND UNTIL DEATH.

WHEN **David finished talking with Saul, Jonathan felt very close to David.** He loved David as much as he loved himself. ²Saul kept David with him from that day on. He did not let David go home to his father's house. ³Jonathan made an agreement with David. He did this because he loved David as much as himself. ⁴He took off his coat and gave it to David. He also gave David his uniform, including his sword, bow and belt. ⁹So Saul watched David closely from then on. He was jealous of him.

Chapter 19Saul told his son Jonathan and all his servants to kill David. But Jonathan cared very much for David. ²So he warned David, "My father Saul is looking for a chance to kill you. Watch out in the morning. Hide in a secret place. ³I will go out and stand with my father in the field where you are hiding. I'll talk to him about you. Then I'll let you know what I find out."

⁴Jonathan talked to Saul his father. He said good things about David. Jonathan said, "You are the king. Don't do wrong to your servant David. He did nothing wrong to you. What he did has helped you greatly. ⁵David risked his life when he killed Goliath the Philistine. The Lord won a great victory for all Israel. You saw it, and you were happy. Why would you do wrong against David? He's innocent. There's no reason to kill him!"

⁶Saul listened to Jonathan. Then he made this promise: "As surely as the Lord lives, David won't be put to death."

From I Samuel 18, 19

I'LL FIND OUT THE TRUTH. NOW, LET'S GO OUT IN THE FIELD WHERE WE CAN SET UP A SECRET PLAN FOR ME TO LET YOU KNOW HOW MY FATHER FEELS.

? What did Jonathan do to protect David?

? Jonathan didn't have to stick up for David. He could have smuggled him out of the country instead. Why do you think Jonathan took the problem right to the king?

? Being a friend means helping someone become the person God has intended him or her to be. Sometimes this means that you may have to step back and let your friend get the glory or as in the case of Jonathan, step in to protect your friend. What is one thing you've done to help a friend?

A friend loves you all the time.
Proverbs 17:17

Which prayer fits you best? Choose one:

Dear God, thank You for the friends You've given me. Help me to encourage them to serve You. Amen.

Dear God, I need a good friend. Help me to be a good friend to those around me so that I can develop a friendship with someone special. Thanks, God. Amen

Morell ▐▐▐▶

THINK ABOUT YOUR
BEST FRIEND.

WHAT DO YOU LIKE
ABOUT HIM OR HER?

WHAT TALENTS OR
ABILITIES DO YOU
THINK GOD HAS GIVEN
YOUR FRIEND?

HOW CAN YOU HELP
YOUR FRIEND PRACTICE
USING HIS OR HER
ABILITIES FOR GOD?

NOW Saul had chased the Philistines away.

Then he was told, "David is in the Desert of En Gedi." ²So he chose 3,000 men from all Israel. He took these men and began looking for David and his men. They looked near the Rocks of the Wild Goats.

³Saul came to the sheep pens beside the road. A cave was there, and he went in to relieve himself. Now David and his men were hiding far back in the cave. ⁴The men said to David, "Today is the day the Lord talked about! The Lord told you, 'I will give your enemy to you. You can do anything you want with him.'"

Then David crawled near Saul. He cut off a corner of Saul's robe. But Saul did not notice him. ⁵Later David felt guilty because he had cut off a corner of Saul's robe. ⁶He said to his men, "May the Lord keep me from doing such a thing to my master! Saul is the Lord's appointed king. I should not do anything against him, because he is the Lord's appointed king!" ⁷David used these words to stop his men. He did not let them attack Saul. Then Saul left the cave and went his way.

⁸When David came out of the cave, he shouted to Saul, "My master and king!" Saul looked back, and David bowed facedown on the ground. ⁹He said to Saul, "Why do you listen when people say, "David plans to harm you'? ¹⁰You have seen something with your own eyes today. You have seen how the Lord put you in my power in the cave. But I refused to kill you. I was merciful to you. I said, "I won't harm my master, because he is the Lord's appointed king.' ¹¹My father, look at this piece of your robe in my hand! I cut off the corner of your robe, but I didn't kill you. Now understand and know I am not planning any evil against you.". . .

¹⁶David finished saying these words. Then Saul asked, "Is that your voice, David my son?" And he cried loudly. ¹⁷He said, "You are right, and I am wrong. . . . May the Lord reward you because you were good to me today. ²⁰I know you will surely be king. You will rule the kingdom of Israel.

HE'S YOUR WIFE'S FATHER— SO IF YOU DON'T WANT TO KILL HIM, I'LL DO IT FOR YOU.

NO— HE WAS CHOSEN BY GOD TO BE OUR KING. IT IS NOT FOR US TO DECIDE WHEN HE WILL DIE.

More!▐▐▐▶

From I Samuel 24

71

AFTER A TIME SAUL LEAVES THE CAVE—AND DAVID CALLS AFTER HIM.

MY LORD THE KING.

DAVI

? What did David's men want him to do?

? What reason did David give for not killing Saul?

? God has placed people over us to teach us and protect us — people like our parents, our pastor, our teachers. God has made them responsible for our souls. To resist the authorities over us goes against God's plan. Think of a time when you went against someone who was in charge. What happened?

Respect those people . . . who lead you in the Lord and teach you. Respect them with a very special love because of the work they do with you.
I Thessalonians 5:12, 13

Lord, sometimes it's hard to always obey those who are put in charge. Give me a willing heart so that I show those over me respect. Amen.

ON THE LEFT SIDE OF THE SPACE BELOW, DRAW A PICTURE OF YOUR FACE WHEN YOU DON'T WANT TO DO WHAT YOUR TEACHER WANTS YOU TO DO. ON THE RIGHT SIDE, DRAW HOW YOU THINK GOD WOULD WANT YOU TO LOOK IN THE SAME SITUATION.

72

I WANT TO GO WITH YOU, ELIJAH.

THE LORD HAS TOLD ME TO GO TO JORDAN. YOU DON'T NEED TO GO ALONG, ELISHA.

IT was near the time for the Lord to take Elijah. He was going to take him by a whirlwind up into heaven. Elijah and Elisha were at Gilgal. ²Elijah said to Elisha, "Please stay here. The Lord has told me to go to Bethel."

But Elisha said, "As the Lord lives, and as you live, I won't leave you."

So they went down to Bethel. . . .

⁴Elijah said to him, "Stay here, because the Lord has sent me to Jericho."

But Elisha said, "As the Lord lives, and as you live, I won't leave you." . . .

So they went to Jericho. . . .

⁶Elijah said to Elisha, "Stay here. The Lord has sent me to the Jordan River."

Elisha answered, "As the Lord lives, and as you live, I won't leave you."

So the two of them went on. ⁷Fifty men from a group of the prophets came. They stood far from where Elijah and Elisha were by the Jordan. ⁸Elijah took off his coat. Then he rolled it up and hit the water. The water divided to the right and to the left. Then Elijah and Elisha crossed over on dry ground.

AFTER they had crossed over,

Elijah said to Elisha, "What can I do for you before I am taken from you?"

¹⁰Elisha said, "Leave me a double share of your spirit."

Elijah said, "You have asked a hard thing. But if you see me when I am taken from you, it will be yours. If you don't, it won't happen."

¹¹Elijah and Elisha were still walking and talking. Then a chariot and horses of fire appeared. The chariot and horses of fire separated Elijah from Elisha. Then Elijah went up to heaven in a whirlwind. ¹²Elisha saw it and shouted, "My father! My father! The chariots of Israel and their horsemen!" Elisha did not see him anymore. Elisha grabbed his own clothes and tore them to show how sad he was.

¹³He picked up Elijah's coat that had fallen from him. Then Elisha returned and stood on the bank of the Jordan. ¹⁴Elisha hit the water with Elijah's coat. He said, "Where is the Lord, the God of Elijah?" When he hit the water, it divided to the right and to the left. Then Elisha crossed over.

From II Kings 2

ELIJAH! ELIJAH! I SEE NOW--THE POWER THAT PROTECTED AND GUIDED YOU IS GREATER THAN ALL THE ARMIES OF EARTH!

74

Whoever helps others will himself be helped.
Proverbs 11:25

Lord, help me to show Your love by being concerned about others. Remind me that if I help others, I will be helped when I am discouraged. Amen.

? Why did Elisha not want to leave Elijah, even for a minute?

? What happened to Elijah?

? Elisha showed concern for Elijah by always being there by his side. Elisha probably knew that he would not receive money as an inheritance from Elijah, yet he wanted the power to do God's work as Elijah had done. Is there someone in your family that you are worried or concerned about? If so, what could you do to help that person?

THINK OF SOMEONE IN YOUR CHURCH WHO NEEDS ENCOURAGEMENT. WRITE OUT THREE SENTENCES THAT COULD CHEER THAT PERSON UP. THEN CALL THAT PERSON ON THE TELEPHONE AND SAY THE WORDS YOU'VE WRITTEN.

Miracle of Oil

> YOUR HUSBAND OWED ME MONEY WHEN HE WAS ALIVE. PAY ME WHAT HE OWED, OR I'LL TAKE YOUR SONS AS SLAVES!

THE wife of a man from a group of the prophets came to Elisha. She said, "Your servant, my husband, is dead! You know he honored the Lord. But now the man he owes money to is coming to take my two boys. He will make them his slaves!"

> THERE, THAT'S THE LAST JAR WE HAVE-- AND MINE IS STILL FULL. IT'S A MIRACLE.

²Elisha answered, "How can I help you? Tell me, what do you have in your house?"

The woman said, "I don't have anything there except a pot of oil."

³Then Elisha said, "Go and get empty jars from all your neighbors. Don't ask for just a few. ⁴Then you must go into your house and close the door. Only you and your sons will be there. Then pour oil into all the jars. Set the full ones to one side."

⁵She left Elisha and shut the door. Only she and her sons were in the house. As they brought the jars to her, she poured the oil. ⁶When the jars were all full, she said to her son, "Bring me another jar."

But he said, "There are no more jars." Then the oil stopped flowing.

⁷She went and told Elisha. Elisha said to her, "Go. Sell the oil and pay what you owe. You and your sons can live on what is left."

From II Kings 4

GOD SAVED US FROM SLAVERY, DIDN'T HE, MOTHER?

YES, THROUGH HIS PROPHET, ELISHA, WHO IS NEVER TOO BUSY TO HELP THOSE OF US WHO NEED HIM.

? What miracle did Elisha do for the woman?

? Why do you think Elisha didn't just give the woman money instead of having her and her children work for it?

? Elisha heard the woman's problem and had compassion for her. Not only did he feel pity, but he went on to help her out of her poverty. When we see people with special needs or problems, we need to do more than feel sorry for them. We need to take action to help. Think of a way that you could encourage someone living in a nursing home or a person who is homeless.

🔑 "This is what the Lord of heaven's armies says: 'Do what is right and fair. Be kind and merciful to each other.'"

Zechariah 7:9

God, help me to think of ways to show compassion to those around me. Help me to remember that because You show compassion for me, I need to show compassion to others. Amen.

Morell ▮▮▶

REMEMBER THE CHOSEN KIDS' CLUB (SEE PAGE 40)? ASK YOUR FRIENDS FOR IDEAS ON HOW YOUR GROUP COULD SHOW COMPASSION TO SOMEONE IN YOUR NEIGHBORHOOD (EXAMPLES: RAKING LEAVES OR SHOVELING SNOW FOR A DISABLED PERSON, BABY-SITTING KIDS IN THE BACKYARD FOR A PARENT WHO NEEDS A BREAK, ETC.). ASK YOUR PARENTS FOR ADVICE AND HELP.

Courage

ESTHER WAS CHOSEN TO BE THE QUEEN OF PERSIA. SHE WAS JEWISH AND HAD NOT TOLD ANYONE HER BACKGROUND. HAMAN, A PERSON OF HIGH RANK IN THE KINGDOM, ORGANIZED AN EVIL PLOT TO DESTROY ALL THE JEWS. ESTHER'S COUSIN MORDECAI WARNED HER BY SENDING A MESSENGER WITH THE NEWS. . . .

THEN Esther told Mordecai . . . [11]"No man or woman may go to the king in the inner courtyard without being called. There is only one law about this. Anyone who enters must be put to death. But if the king holds out his gold scepter, that person may live. And I have not been called to go to the king for 30 days."

[12]And Esther's message was given to Mordecai. [13]Then Mordecai gave orders to say to Esther: "Just because you live in the king's palace, don't think that out of all the Jews you alone will escape. [14]You might keep quiet at this time. Then someone else will help and save the Jews. But you and your father's family will all die. And who knows, you may have been chosen queen for just such a time as this."

[15]Then Esther sent this answer to Mordecai: [16]"Go and get all the Jews in Susa together. For my sake, give up eating. Do not eat or drink for three days, night and day. I and my servant girls will also give up eating. Then I will go to the king, even though it is against the law. And if I die, I die."

A Queen Risks Her Life

SURPRISED AS HE IS BY HER SUDDEN APPEARANCE, THE KING IS PLEASED AT THE SIGHT OF HIS BEAUTIFUL QUEEN. HE HOLDS OUT HIS SCEPTOR TO SHOW THAT SHE IS FORGIVEN, AND ASKS WHAT SHE WANTS.

I ASK THAT YOU AND HAMAN COME TO A DINNER THAT I SHALL PREPARE FOR YOU.

So the king and Haman went in to eat with Queen **Esther.** ²They were drinking wine. And the king said to Esther on this second day also, "What are you asking for? I will give it to you. What is it you want? I will give you as much as half of my kingdom."

³Then Queen Esther answered, "My king, I hope you are pleased with me. If it pleases you, let me live. This is what I ask. And let my people live, too. This is what I want. ⁴I ask this because my people and I have been sold to be destroyed. We are to be killed and completely wiped out. . . ."

⁵Then King Xerxes asked Queen Esther, "Who is he? Where is he? Who has done such a thing?"

⁶Esther said, "A man who is against us! Our enemy is this wicked Haman!"

Then Haman was filled with terror before the king and queen. . . . ⁹Harbona was one of the eunuchs there serving the king. He said, "Look, a platform for hanging people stands near Haman's house. It is 75 feet high. This is the one Haman had prepared for Mordecai, who gave the warning that saved the king."

The king said, "Hang Haman on it!" ¹⁰So they hanged Haman on the platform he had prepared for Mordecai. *From Esther 4, 7*

? What might have happened to Esther if the king wouldn't have extended his scepter to her?

? Mordecai reminded Esther that she, too, was a Jew and would die. But what wonderful opportunity did he present to Esther?

? What a choice!—Die because of the order or die because the king wouldn't accept her presence in the throne room. It took a lot of courage for Esther to go before the king. Think of someone you know or have read about who showed a lot of courage in the face of danger. What was the choice he or she had to face? How did the situation turn out?

MORDECAI IS YOUR COUSIN? I'LL PUT HIM IN HAMAN'S PLACE --SECOND IN POWER IN ALL OF MY KINGDOM. WITH HAMAN OUT OF THE WAY, NO ONE WILL DARE TO HARM EITHER OF YOU.

Have courage. May the Lord be with those who do what is right.

II Chronicles 19:11

Lord, help me to have the courage to stand up for what's right. Give me the strength I need to go against friends when I know they want to do wrong. Amen.

ESTHER TOOK THE RISK EVEN THOUGH SHE KNEW THINGS MIGHT NOT WORK OUT AS SHE PLANNED. THINK OF A SITUATION WHERE YOU MIGHT NEED TO GO AGAINST SOMEONE TO TAKE A STAND FOR RIGHT. SOME EXAMPLES ARE:
WHEN BIGGER KIDS ARE
HASSLING A SMALLER KID
AND YOU NEED TO STEP
IN, WHEN SOMEONE WANTS
TO SHOPLIFT A CANDY
BAR AND YOU DON'T WANT
TO BE A PART OF THE
ACTION, OR WHEN A
FRIEND WANTS TO
CHEAT ON A TEST AND
YOU DON'T THINK IT'S
RIGHT. DRAW A
PICTURE OF HOW
YOU WOULD HANDLE
THE SITUATION.

I'd Rather Eat Vegetables

DANIEL **decided not to eat the king's food and wine** because that would make him unclean. So he asked Ashpenaz for permission not to make himself unclean in this way.

9God made Ashpenaz want to be kind and merciful to Daniel. 10But Ashpenaz said to Daniel, "I am afraid of my master, the king. He ordered me to give you this food and drink. If you don't eat this food, you will begin to look worse than other young men your age. The king will see this. And he will cut off my head because of you."

11Ashpenaz had ordered a guard to watch Daniel, Hananiah, Mishael and Azariah. 12Daniel said to the guard, "Please give us this test for ten days: Don't give us anything but vegetables to eat and water to drink. 13Then after ten days compare us with the other young men who eat the king's food. See for yourself who looks healthier. Then you judge for yourself how you want to treat us, your servants."

14So the guard agreed to test them for ten days. 15After ten days they looked very healthy. They looked better than all of the young men who ate the king's food. 16So the guard took away the king's special food and wine. He gave Daniel, Hananiah, Mishael and Azariah vegetables instead.

17God gave these four men wisdom and the ability to learn. They learned many kinds of things people had written and studied. Daniel could also understand all kinds of visions and dreams.

18The end of the three years came. And Ashpenaz brought all of the young men to King Nebuchadnezzar. 19The king talked to them. He found that none of the young men were as good as Daniel, Hananiah, Mishael and Azariah. So those four young men became the king's servants. 20Every time the king asked them about something important, they showed much wisdom and understanding.

From Daniel 1

More!▶

GIVE US A TEN-DAY TRIAL. LET US EAT OUR FOOD AND THEN SEE IF WE ARE NOT STRONGER THAN THE OTHERS.

BUT IT'S THE KING'S ORDER -- WE DARE NOT DISOBEY. I LIKE YOU, DANIEL, BUT I DON'T WANT TO GET INTO TROUBLE.

THE TEST IS MADE, AND AT THE END OF TEN DAYS, THERE'S NO DOUBT--DANIEL AND HIS FRIENDS NOT ONLY **LOOK** STRONGER, THEY **ARE** STRONGER.

AT THE END OF THREE YEARS, THE YOUNG MEN ARE BROUGHT BEFORE THE KING. HE TALKS WITH EACH ONE, THEN MAKES HIS DECISION.

I HAVE CHOSEN THESE FOUR--DANIEL, SHADRACH, MESHACH, AND ABEDNEGO-- TO SERVE AS MY ADVISERS.

THERE IS NONE TO EQUAL THEM, SIR.

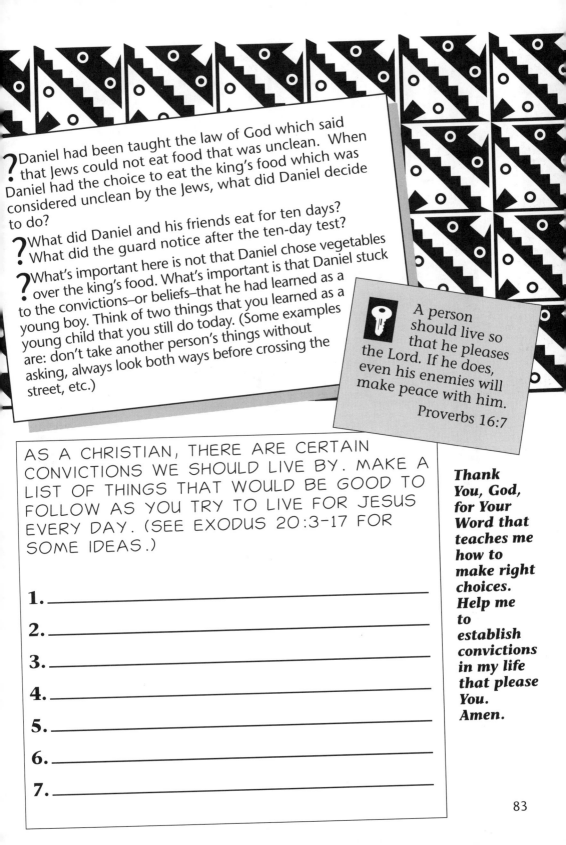

? Daniel had been taught the law of God which said that Jews could not eat food that was unclean. When Daniel had the choice to eat the king's food which was considered unclean by the Jews, what did Daniel decide to do?

? What did Daniel and his friends eat for ten days? What did the guard notice after the ten-day test?

? What's important here is not that Daniel chose vegetables over the king's food. What's important is that Daniel stuck to the convictions–or beliefs–that he had learned as a young boy. Think of two things that you learned as a young child that you still do today. (Some examples are: don't take another person's things without asking, always look both ways before crossing the street, etc.)

A person should live so that he pleases the Lord. If he does, even his enemies will make peace with him.
Proverbs 16:7

AS A CHRISTIAN, THERE ARE CERTAIN CONVICTIONS WE SHOULD LIVE BY. MAKE A LIST OF THINGS THAT WOULD BE GOOD TO FOLLOW AS YOU TRY TO LIVE FOR JESUS EVERY DAY. (SEE EXODUS 20:3-17 FOR SOME IDEAS.)

1. _____
2. _____
3. _____
4. _____
5. _____
6. _____
7. _____

Thank You, God, for Your Word that teaches me how to make right choices. Help me to establish convictions in my life that please You. Amen.

83

A Very Hot Spot

MUSIC FILLS THE AIR-- SOLEMNLY THE OFFICIALS OF BABYLON BOW DOWN AND WORSHIP THE GOLDEN STATUE--ALL BUT SHADRACH, MESHACH, AND ABEDNEGO.

SEE? THEY REFUSE TO BOW DOWN!

THE KING became very angry. . . .

[16]Shadrach, Meshach and Abednego answered the king. They said, "Nebuchadnezzar, we do not need to defend ourselves to you. [17]You can throw us into the blazing furnace. The God we serve is able to save us from the furnace and your power. If he does this, it is good. [18]But even if God does not save us, we want you, our king, to know this: We will not serve your gods. We will not worship the gold statue you have set up."

[19]Then Nebuchadnezzar was furious with Shadrach, Meshach and Abednego. He ordered the furnace to be heated seven times hotter than usual. [20]Then he commanded some of the strongest soldiers in his army to tie up Shadrach, Meshach and Abednego. The king told the soldiers to throw them into the blazing furnace.

[21]So Shadrach, Meshach and Abednego were tied up and thrown into the blazing furnace. They were still wearing their robes, trousers, turbans and other clothes. [22]The king was very angry when he gave the command. And the furnace was made very hot. The fire was so hot that the flames killed the strong soldiers who took Shadrach, Meshach and Abednego there. [23]Firmly tied, Shadrach, Meshach and Abednego fell into the blazing furnace.

From Daniel 3

? Do you think it was hard for the three Hebrews to keep standing when everyone else was bowing down to the statue? Why or why not?

? Were they sure that God would keep them from burning up? How do you know?

? Sometimes being committed to God means having to stand alone when you're with friends at school. Can you think of a time when your friends wanted to do something you knew would get you in trouble? How did you feel? Did you stand up to them or did you do what they wanted to do?

Teach me to do what you want, because you are my God. Let your good Spirit lead me on level ground.

Psalm 143:10

God, thank You for being there when I need You. Help me to commit myself to You and stand firm on the teachings of Your Word. Amen.

Morе▐▐▶

WE WORSHIP GOD BY DOING DIFFERENT THINGS. WE BUILD OUR RELATIONSHIP WITH GOD ONE STEP AT A TIME. LOOK AT THE LIST BELOW. CHECK ONE THING THAT YOU WILL PROMISE TO DO FOR GOD THIS WEEK.

LORD, THIS WEEK I WILL: (CHECK ONE)

❑ READ FIVE VERSES IN MY BIBLE EVERY DAY.
☑ TALK TO YOU IN PRAYER FIVE MINUTES EVERY DAY.
❑ EARN MONEY BY DOING AN EXTRA JOB AND THEN GIVE IT IN THE OFFERING NEXT SUNDAY.
❑ OBEY MY PARENTS WITHOUT ARGUING OR TALKING BACK THIS WEEK.
❑ OTHER IDEAS I HAVE:

_____

_____

_____

YOUR SPECIAL KID,

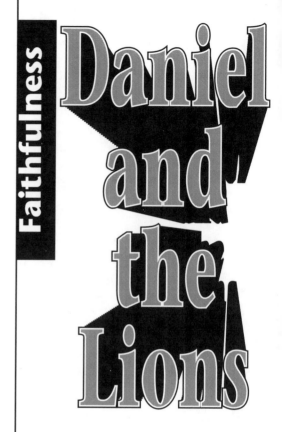

Faithfulness

Daniel and the Lions

DANIEL WAS FAITHFUL TO GOD. THREE TIMES EACH DAY HE WOULD PRAY. THE MEN HE WORKED WITH WERE JEALOUS OF HIS GOOD RECORD AND WANTED TO GET HIM IN TROUBLE WITH THE BOSS, KING DARIUS. BUT DANIEL WAS TRUSTWORTHY AND A GOOD WORKER. SO THE MEN PLOTTED AGAINST HIM AND HAD THE KING SIGN AN ORDER THAT NO ONE COULD PRAY TO ANY GOD BUT THE KING'S GOD. BUT THAT DIDN'T STOP DANIEL FROM PRAYING TO HIS GOD. . . .

A FEW MINUTES LATER DANIEL, WHO BROKE THE KING'S LAW BY PRAYING TO GOD, IS CAST INTO THE LIONS' DEN.

MAY THE GOD WHOM YOU SERVE PROTECT YOU.

KING Darius . . . did not eat that night. He did not have any

entertainment brought to entertain him. And he could not sleep.

19The next morning King Darius got up at dawn. He hurried to the lions' den. 20As he came near the den, he was worried. He called out to Daniel. He said, "Daniel, servant of the living God! Has your God that you always worship been able to save you from the lions?"

21Daniel answered, "My king, live forever! 22My God sent his angel to close the lions' mouths. They have not hurt me, because my God knows I am innocent. I never did anything wrong to you, my king."

23King Darius was very happy. He told his servants to lift Daniel out of the lions' den. So they lifted him out and did not find any injury on him. This was because Daniel had trusted in his God.

25Then King Darius wrote a letter. It was to all people and all nations, to those who spoke every language in the world:

I wish you great wealth.

26I am making a new law. This law is for people in every part of my kingdom. All of you must fear and respect the God of Daniel.

Daniel's God is the living God.
    He lives forever.
His kingdom will never be destroyed.
    His rule will never end.
27God rescues and saves people.
    God does mighty miracles
    in heaven and on earth.
God saved Daniel
    from the power of the lions.

From Daniel 6

MY GOD HAS SHUT THE LIONS' MOUTHS!

? What did Daniel do to show faithfulness to God?

? God showed faithfulness to Daniel by helping him. What did God do?

? Showing faithfulness means that a person can be counted on to do a certain thing. For instance, God could count on Daniel to pray three times each day. Can your parents count on you to do a certain job every day (or almost every day!)? What is that job?

If you are faithful, I will give you the crown of life.
Revelation 2:10b

Dear God, thank You for always being there when I need to talk to someone. Help me to show my love for You by being faithful in the things I do for You and others. Amen.

WHAT ARE WAYS THAT WE CAN BE FAITHFUL TO GOD? SOME EXAMPLES WOULD BE GOING TO CHURCH EVERY SUNDAY, PRAYING AND READING GOD'S WORD, BEING NICE TO OTHERS. . . . THE LIST COULD GO ON AND ON. DRAW A PICTURE OF ONE WAY THAT YOU CAN SHOW YOUR LOVE FOR GOD EVERY DAY.

A Gift from a Stable

MARY gave birth to her first son. There were no rooms left in the inn. So she wrapped the baby with cloths and laid him in a box where animals are fed.

8That night, some shepherds were in the fields nearby watching their sheep. 9An angel of the Lord stood before them. The glory of the Lord was shining around them, and suddenly they became very frightened. 10The angel said to them, "Don't be afraid, because I am bringing you some good news. It will be a joy to all the people. 11Today your Savior was born in David's town. He is Christ, the Lord. 12This is how you will know him: You will find a baby wrapped in cloths and lying in a feeding box." 13Then a very large group of angels from heaven joined the first angel. All the angels were praising God.

From Luke 2

More⟶

THEN THE SKY IS FILLED WITH A GREAT CHOIR OF ANGELS -- SINGING THEIR PRAISE TO GOD.

Glory to God in the highest, and on earth peace, good will toward men.

? What do people do immediately before a baby is born? What might friends and relatives do for the new baby?

? Do you think that Mary might have wondered if something was wrong with the plan when she had to have her baby in a stable?

? The Bible tells us in Romans 6:23, "But God gives us a free gift—life forever in Christ Jesus our Lord." Jesus was the greatest gift that God gave the world. When Jesus was older He took all our sins and paid for them by shedding His blood on the cross. Now we have the chance to live with Him forever in heaven.

AN ANGEL TOLD US THAT THE SAVIOR HAS BEEN BORN. MAY WE SEE HIM?

Thanks, God, for loving me so much that You made a way for me to live with You forever. Help me to love You more each day, and serve You with my words and actions. Amen.

"She will give birth to a son. You will name the son Jesus. Give him that name because he will save his people from their sins."

Matthew 1:21

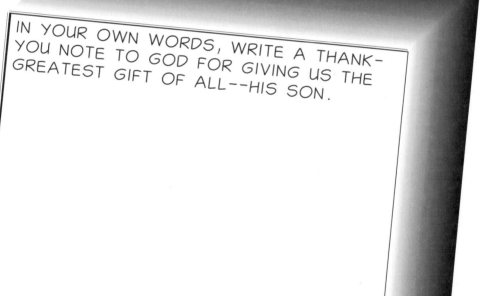

IN YOUR OWN WORDS, WRITE A THANK-YOU NOTE TO GOD FOR GIVING US THE GREATEST GIFT OF ALL--HIS SON.

Worshiping with Gifts

IT IS A SIGN FROM GOD THAT THE GREAT KING OF THE JEWS HAS BEEN BORN.

LET US GO TO JERUSALEM AND FIND THE KING.

JESUS was born in the town of Bethlehem in Judea during the time when Herod was king. After Jesus was born, some wise men from the east came to Jerusalem. ²They asked, "Where is the baby who was born to be the king of the Jews? We saw his star in the east. We came to worship him."

³When King Herod heard about this new king of the Jews, he was troubled. And all the people in Jerusalem were worried too. ⁴Herod called a meeting of all the leading priests and teachers of the law. He asked them where the Christ would be born. ⁵They answered, "In the town of Bethlehem in Judea. The prophet wrote about this in the Scriptures:

⁶'But you, Bethlehem, in the land of Judah,
you are important among the rulers of Judah.
A ruler will come from you.
He will be like a shepherd for my people, the Israelites.'"

. . . ⁹The wise men heard the king and then left. They saw the same star they had seen in the east. It went before them until it stopped above the place where the child was. ¹⁰When the wise men saw the star, they were filled with joy. ¹¹They went to the house where the child was and saw him with his mother, Mary. They bowed down and worshiped the child. They opened the gifts they brought for him. They gave him treasures of gold, frankincense, and myrrh.

From Matthew 2

IS THERE ANYTHING IN THE SACRED BOOKS TELLING ABOUT A BABY WHO WILL BECOME KING OF THE JEWS?

YES, THE SCRIPTURES SAY HE WILL BE BORN IN BETHLEHEM.

? The wise men worshiped Jesus by kneeling before Him and giving Him expensive gifts. God doesn't expect us to do the same. Why?

? Have you ever really wanted to talk to God but felt awkward because of the place you were in or the people you were with? What are some ways to worship God other than speaking words in a prayer? (Examples: helping others, singing praise songs, telling others about Jesus, etc.)

? One way the wise men worshiped was by each giving the baby a different gift. Each of us has different gifts and talents that we can give to God as worship. Name two things that you could give as worship to God.

Thank You, God, for always being there when I want to talk to You. Help me to think of ways that I can show You how much I love You. Amen.

Praise the Lord for the glory of his name. Worship the Lord because he is holy.

Psalm 29:2

WE HAVE COME A LONG WAY TO WOR-SHIP THE ROYAL CHILD.

AND TO BRING HIM GIFTS OF GOLD, FRANKINCENSE, AND MYRRH.

More!

WE CAN WORSHIP GOD
IN MANY WAYS. WE CAN
PRAISE HIM WITH OUR
WORDS AND WITH OUR
ACTIONS. DRAW ONE
WAY THAT YOU CAN
WORSHIP GOD.

Purposefulness

BOY in the TEMPLE

JOSEPH, WHERE IS JESUS?

HE'S WITH HIS FRIENDS. I'LL FIND HIM.

EVERY year Jesus' parents went to Jerusalem

for the Passover Feast. 42When Jesus was 12 years old, they went to the feast as they always did. 43When the feast days were over, they went home. The boy Jesus stayed behind in Jerusalem, but his parents did not know it. 44Joseph and Mary traveled for a whole day. They thought that Jesus was with them in the group. Then they began to look for him among their family and friends, 45but they did not find him. So they went back to Jerusalem to look for him there. 46After three days they found him. Jesus was sitting in the Temple with the religious teachers, listening to them and asking them questions. 47All who heard him were amazed at his understanding and wise answers. 48When Jesus' parents saw him, they were amazed. His mother said to him, "Son, why did you do this to us? Your father and I were very worried about you. We have been looking for you."

49Jesus asked, "Why did you have to look for me? You should have known that I must be where my Father's work is!" 50But they did not understand the meaning of what he said.

51Jesus went with them to Nazareth and obeyed them. His mother was still thinking about all that had happened. 52Jesus continued to learn more and more and to grow physically. People liked him, and he pleased God.

From Luke 2

Morel

? Do you think that Jesus intended to hide from His parents? Why or why not?

? Why did Jesus stay at the temple so long?

? Jesus had a purpose in talking to the teachers — He wanted to learn more about God's work. If you could be anything you wanted to be in God's work — a teacher, minister, musician, missionary, choir director, etc. — what would you like to be? Why?

In all the work you are doing, work the best you can. Work as if you were working for the Lord, not for men.
Colossians 3:23

Dear Lord, help me to set a goal to serve You with my whole heart. And then give me strength each day to keep working toward that goal. Amen.

A TRACK RUNNER DOESN'T DECIDE TO SIT DOWN AND EAT A SANDWICH IN THE MIDDLE OF A RACE. HE SETS HIS EYES ON THE FINISH LINE AND DOESN'T QUIT UNTIL HE REACHES IT. WE WOULD SAY THAT RUNNER IS PURPOSEFUL. THINK OF A GOAL YOU WOULD LIKE TO REACH THIS WEEK (GETTING AN ASSIGNMENT DONE, DOING A JOB FOR SOMEONE ELSE, EARNING EXTRA MONEY, ETC.) WHAT WILL IT TAKE FOR YOU TO REACH THAT GOAL?

No More Wine!

Two ^{days} **later there was a wedding in the town of Cana** in Galilee. Jesus' mother was there. [2]Jesus and his followers were also invited to the wedding. [3]When all the wine was gone, Jesus' mother said to him, "They have no more wine."

DURING THE FEAST MARY DISCOVERS SOMETHING THAT WILL EMBARRASS THE GROOM -- THERE IS NO MORE WINE. SHE TELLS JESUS, THEN SHE GOES TO THE SERVANTS.

DO WHATEVER HE TELLS YOU.

[4]Jesus answered, "Dear woman, why come to me? My time has not yet come."

[5]His mother said to the servants, "Do whatever he tells you to do."

[6]In that place there were six stone water jars. The Jews used jars like these in their washing ceremony. Each jar held about 20 or 30 gallons.

[7]Jesus said to the servants, "Fill the jars with water." So they filled the jars to the top.

[8]Then he said to them, "Now take some out and give it to the master of the feast."

So the servants took the water to the master. [9]When he tasted it, the water had become wine. He did not know where the wine came from. But the servants who brought the water knew. The master of the wedding called the bridegroom [10]and said to him, "People always serve the best wine first. Later, after the guests have been drinking a lot, they serve the cheaper wine. But you have saved the best wine till now."

From John 2

FILL THESE JARS WITH WATER.

WHY WATER? IT'S WINE WE NEED.

? What did Jesus do to help the master of the feast?

? Besides providing something more to drink, what was special about the wine in the six jars?

? Helping others is something that pleases God and can be done by people of all ages—young and old. Think of a time when you helped someone. How did your helping make his or her job easier?

BUT THE SERVANTS SENSE A STRANGE AUTHORITY IN JESUS, AND THEY OBEY HIM.

NOW TAKE SOME TO THE HEADWAITER.

WHY—IT IS WINE! IT'S A MIRACLE!

THIS MAN MUST BE A PROPHET OF GOD—NO ORDINARY MAN COULD DO SUCH A THING!

He will not forget the work you
did and the love you showed for
him by helping his people. And
he will remember that you are still
helping them.

Hebrews 6:10

*Dear God, help me to see the
needs of people who need Your
help. Then show me ways to
help them. Amen.*

WHAT IS ONE THING YOU COULD DO TO
HELP SOMEONE THIS WEEK? DRAW A
PICTURE OF YOU AS YOU GIVE THAT HELP.

A Late-Night Talk

NICODEMUS, A JUDGE OF THE JEWISH SUPREME COURT, HAS A PROBLEM HE CAN'T SOLVE. PEOPLE IN JERUSALEM ARE ASKING, "IS JESUS THE SAVIOR WHO WILL OVERTHROW THE ROMANS AND SET UP GOD'S KINGDOM IN PALESTINE?"

NICODEMUS ISN'T SURE, AND HE WONDERS: "WHAT MUST A MAN DO TO ENTER GOD'S KINGDOM?" HE HAS TO FIND OUT. SO SECRETLY-- BY NIGHT-- HE GOES TO THE PLACE WHERE JESUS IS STAYING, AND JESUS ANSWERS HIS QUESTION EVEN BEFORE HE ASKS IT...

A MAN MUST BE BORN OVER AGAIN TO ENTER GOD'S KINGDOM.

BORN AGAIN? HOW CAN I BE BORN AGAIN WHEN I AM OLD?

THERE

was a man named Nicodemus who was one of the Pharisees. He was an important Jewish leader. ²One night Nicodemus came to Jesus. He said, "Teacher, we know that you are a teacher sent from God. No one can do the miracles you do, unless God is with him."

³Jesus answered, "I tell you the truth. Unless one is born again, he cannot be in God's kingdom."

⁴Nicodemus said, "But if a man is already old, how can he be born again? He cannot enter his mother's body again. So how can he be born a second time?"

⁵But Jesus answered, "I tell you the truth. Unless one is born from water and the Spirit, he cannot enter God's kingdom. ⁶A person's body is born from his human parents. But a person's spiritual life is born from the Spirit. ⁷Don't be surprised when I tell you, 'You must all be born again.' ⁸The wind blows where it wants to go. You hear the wind blow. But you don't know where the wind comes from or where it is going. It is the same with every person who is born from the Spirit."

⁹Nicodemus asked, "How can all this be possible?"

¹⁰Jesus said, "You are an important teacher in Israel. But you still don't understand these things? ¹¹I tell you the truth. We talk about what we know. We tell about what we have seen. But you don't accept what we tell you. ¹²I have told you about things here on earth, but you do not believe me. So surely you will not believe me if I tell you about the things of heaven! ¹³The only one who has ever gone up to heaven is the One who came down from heaven—the Son of Man. . . .

¹⁶"For God loved the world so much that he gave his only Son. God gave his Son so that whoever believes in him may not be lost, but have eternal life.

From John 3

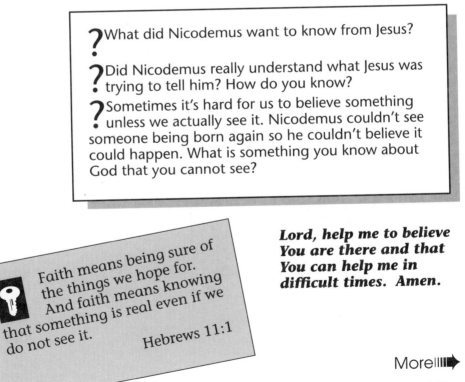

? What did Nicodemus want to know from Jesus?

? Did Nicodemus really understand what Jesus was trying to tell him? How do you know?

? Sometimes it's hard for us to believe something unless we actually see it. Nicodemus couldn't see someone being born again so he couldn't believe it could happen. What is something you know about God that you cannot see?

Faith means being sure of the things we hope for. And faith means knowing that something is real even if we do not see it.

Hebrews 11:1

Lord, help me to believe You are there and that You can help me in difficult times. Amen.

More ➡

WHEN IT'S HARD TO BELIEVE THAT GOD IS THERE TO HELP YOU, READ BIBLE VERSES OUT LOUD. AS YOUR EARS HEAR GOD'S WORDS, YOUR FAITH IN HIM WILL GROW AND YOU WILL BE ENCOURAGED. LOOK UP THESE VERSES AND READ THEM OUT LOUD. THEN WRITE WHAT THE VERSE MEANS TO YOU.

⇨ DEUTERONOMY 31:6
GOD WILL NEVER LEAVE ME OR FORGET ABOUT ME.
⇨ PSALM 46:1

⇨ ISAIAH 41:13

⇨ JOHN 14:13

⇨ I PETER 5:7

A JEW! DO
HE KNOW
AREN'T WEL
IN SAMAR

Talk of the Town

IN Samaria Jesus came to the town called Sychar. This town is near the field that Jacob gave to his son Joseph. [6]Jacob's well was there. Jesus was tired from his long trip. So he sat down beside the well. It was about noon. [7]A Samaritan woman came to the well to get some water. Jesus said to her, "Please give me a drink." [8](This happened while Jesus' followers were in town buying some food.)

[9]The woman said, "I am surprised that you ask me for a drink. You are a Jew and I am a Samaritan." (Jews are not friends with Samaritans.)

[10]Jesus said, "You don't know what God gives. And you don't know who asked you for a drink. If you knew, you would have asked me, and I would have given you living water."

[11]The woman said, "Sir, where will you get that living water? The well is very deep, and you have nothing to get water with. [12]Are you greater than Jacob, our father? Jacob is the one who gave us this well. He drank from it himself. Also, his sons and flocks drank from this well."

[13]Jesus answered, "Every person who drinks this water will be thirsty again. [14]But whoever drinks the water I give will never be thirsty again. The water I give will become a spring of water flowing inside him. It will give him eternal life."

[15]The woman said to him, "Sir, give me this water. Then I will never be thirsty again. And I will not have to come back here to get more water."

. . .[25]The woman said, "I know that the Messiah is coming." (Messiah is the One called Christ.) "When the Messiah comes, he will explain everything to us."

[26]Then Jesus said, "He is talking to you now. I am he."

. . .[28]Then the woman left her water jar and went back to town. She said to the people, [29]"A man told me everything I have ever done. Come see him. Maybe he is the Christ!" [30]So the people left the town and went to see Jesus.

From John 4

Did the woman understand what the "living water" was that Jesus spoke of? What makes you think so? What happened when the woman realized that Jesus was the Messiah she had been looking for? When the woman heard all that Jesus said, she got excited. She ran into town and told everybody. Her enthusiasm was contagious because all the people came out to see the man she spoke of. How do you react when you are really excited about something?

COME! SEE A MAN WHO HAS TOLD ME THINGS ABOUT MY LIFE THAT NO STRANGER COULD KNOW. HE IS THE PROMISED MESSIAH! THE SAVIOR!

I can do all things through Christ because he gives me strength.
Philippians 4:13

Dear God, thank You for giving me strength each day to do the things required of me. Help me to work cheerfully and with enthusiasm because I know that everything I do is for You. Amen.

DRAW TWO CIRCLES. IN THE CIRCLE ON THE LEFT, DRAW A PICTURE OF YOUR FACE AS YOU USUALLY LOOK WHEN MOM OR DAD HAS A JOB FOR YOU TO DO. ON THE RIGHT, DRAW A PICTURE OF YOUR FACE WHEN YOU ARE REALLY ENTHUSED AND EXCITED ABOUT SOMETHING. DO THE TWO FACES MATCH? HOW CAN YOU SHOW MORE ENTHUSIASM FOR THE JOBS PEOPLE ASK YOU TO DO?

THROUGH the Roof

So **many people gathered to hear him preach that the house was full.** There was no place to stand, not even outside the door. Jesus was teaching them. 3Some people came, bringing a paralyzed man to Jesus. Four of them were carrying the paralyzed man. 4But they could not get to Jesus because of the crowd. So they went to the roof above Jesus and made a hole in the roof. Then they lowered the mat with the paralyzed man on it. 5Jesus saw that these men had great faith. So he said to the paralyzed man, "Young man, your sins are forgiven."

6Some of the teachers of the law were sitting there. They saw what Jesus did, and they said to themselves, 7"Why does this man say things like that? He is saying things that are against God. Only God can forgive sins."

8At once Jesus knew what these teachers of the law were thinking. So he said to them, "Why are you thinking these things? 9Which is easier: to tell this paralyzed man, 'Your sins are forgiven,' or to tell him, 'Stand up. Take your mat and walk'? 10But I will prove to you that the Son of Man has authority on earth to forgive sins." So Jesus said to the paralyzed man, 11"I tell you, stand up. Take your mat and go home." 12 Immediately the paralyzed man stood up. He took his mat and walked out while everyone was watching him.

The people were amazed and praised God. They said, "We have never seen anything like this!"

From Mark 2

What might the four men have thought when they saw such a large crowd outside the house where Jesus was teaching?

In this story, who had great faith—the paralyzed man or his friends?

Being a responsible person means that you are willing to do what you say you'll do. The four men didn't give up when they saw the large crowd, but took the responsibility to get their friend to Jesus. Think of an instance when you took responsibility for a friend — perhaps you promised to have your parents pick him up, help with homework, etc. How did it make you feel to help?

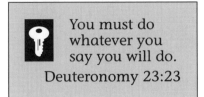

You must do whatever you say you will do.
Deuteronomy 23:23

Lord, help me to be responsible about the words I say and the things I do. Remind me to keep the promises I make. Amen.

WHAT YOU SAY IS SO IMPORTANT. PEOPLE EXPECT YOU TO KEEP YOUR WORD. IF YOU DON'T, THEY THINK THAT YOU ARE NOT A RESPONSIBLE PERSON. SOMETIMES WE BREAK OUR PROMISE AND NEED TO ASK FORGIVENESS, BUT GOD WANTS US TO KEEP TRYING TO IMPROVE. HERE IS A WAY TO START. FILL OUT THIS RESPONSIBILITY CARD.

I MADE A PROMISE TO _____

TO DO THE FOLLOWING: _____

_____

_____

I COMPLETED IT ON _____

SIGNED: _____

A Job Well Done for No $$$

JESUS **left there and went into their synagogue.** [10]In the synagogue, there was a man with a crippled hand. Some Jews there were looking for a reason to accuse Jesus of doing wrong. So they asked him, "Is it right to heal on the Sabbath day?"

[11]Jesus answered, "If any of you has a sheep, and it falls into a ditch on the Sabbath day, then you will take the sheep and help it out of the ditch. [12]Surely a man is more important than a sheep. So the law of Moses allows people to do good things on the Sabbath day."

[13]Then Jesus said to the man with the crippled hand, "Let me see your hand." The man put his hand out, and the hand became well again, the same as the other hand. [14]But the Pharisees left and made plans to kill Jesus.

From Matthew 12

LOOK--JESUS IS TALKING TO THAT MAN WITH THE WITHERED HAND. LET'S SEE IF WE CAN CATCH HIM BREAKING A SABBATH LAW. THEN WE'LL HAVE A CASE AGAINST HIM.

IS IT LAWFUL TO HEAL ON THE SABBATH?

IF ONE OF YOU HAD A SHEEP THAT FELL INTO A PIT ON THE SABBATH, WOULDN'T YOU LIFT IT OUT? ISN'T A MAN MORE VALUABLE THAN A SHEEP? THE ANSWER TO YOUR QUESTION IS-- YES, IT IS LAWFUL TO DO GOOD ON THE SABBATH.

THEN, BEFORE ALL THE PHARISEES, JESUS TELLS THE MAN TO HOLD OUT HIS HAND. AND AS HE DOES...

MY HAND -- IT IS STRONG AGAIN.' GOD HAS ANSWERED MY PRAYERS.'

? What was Jesus trying to prove to the Pharisees?

? Did Jesus heal the man because He knew that the man would pay Him BIG BUCKS to have his hand made well?

? Jesus did a lot of good things for people. He didn't expect payment. Think of two things that you've done in the last month where you did it just because you wanted to be nice to someone.

 So love your enemies. Do good to them, and lend to them without hoping to get anything back.

Luke 6:35

Dear God, help me get ideas for doing good things for others that will please You. Thanks. Amen.

Morell

IN TODAY'S WORLD EVERYONE EXPECTS TO GET PAID FOR EVERYTHING THEY DO. BUT JESUS TOLD US TO DO GOOD THINGS EVEN TO OUR ENEMIES. THAT'S A TALL ORDER! PAYMENT DOESN'T ALWAYS COME IN THE FORM OF DOLLARS AND CENTS. THINGS LIKE FRIENDSHIP, HAVING OTHERS RESPECT YOU, AND HAVING GOD SEE THAT WE'RE PRACTICING HIS INSTRUCTIONS CAN BE ADDED BENEFITS. COMPLETE THE FOLLOWING STATEMENT. ON THE DATE OF

_____

I, _____
DID SOMETHING GOOD FOR _____

THE THING I DID WAS:

_____

I RECEIVED NO PAY, BUT I THINK THE BENEFITS TO ME FOR DOING THIS JOB WERE:

WHEN I DID THIS, I WAS PRACTICING GOD'S GOODNESS.

SIGNED, _____

IT'S THE KIND OF A NIGHT WHEN A SUDDEN STORM COULD HIT.

Caught in a Storm

THAT evening, Jesus said to his followers, "Come with me across the lake." 36He and the followers left the people there. They went in the boat that Jesus was already sitting in. There were also other boats with them. 37A very strong wind came up on the lake. The waves began coming over the sides and into the boat. It was almost full of water. 38Jesus was at the back of the boat, sleeping with his head on a pillow. The followers went to him and woke him. They said, "Teacher, do you care about us? We will drown!"

39Jesus stood up and commanded the wind and the waves to stop. He said, "Quiet! Be still!" Then the wind stopped, and the lake became calm.

40Jesus said to his followers, "Why are you afraid? Do you still have no faith?"

41The followers were very afraid and asked each other, "What kind of man is this? Even the wind and the waves obey him!"

From Mark 4

Morell

111

? Why were the disciples afraid?

? What was Jesus doing at the back of the boat? When the disciples talked to Him, what did Jesus do about the storm?

? Peacefulness is the sense of feeling at rest even though you may be going through some difficult things. Every day we face things that seem to take our peace away. What are some things that keep you from being at peace? Some examples could be: fighting with your brother, being bullied by someone at school, etc.

PEACE, BE STILL!

Dear God, thank You for being there when I feel I have no peace in my life. Remind me that even when things go wrong, You are always there for me. Amen.

I pray that the God who gives hope will fill you with much joy and peace while you trust in him.
Romans 15:13

DRAW AN OUTLINE OF A BOAT WITH JESUS AND YOU INSIDE. AROUND THE BOAT DRAW BIG WAVES AND WRITE THINGS IN THE WATER THAT TAKE AWAY YOUR PEACE--ANGER, JEALOUSY, PROBLEMS, FIGHTING, ETC. WHEN YOU FEEL THAT YOU HAVE NO PEACE, TURN TO THIS PAGE AND REMIND YOURSELF THAT JESUS IS ALWAYS THERE WITH YOU.

A small Answer to a Big Problem

AFTER this, Jesus went across Lake Galilee (or, Lake Tiberias). ²Many people followed him because they saw the miracles he did to heal the sick. ³Jesus went up on a hill and there sat down with his followers. ⁴It was almost the time for the Jewish Passover Feast.

⁵Jesus looked up and saw a large crowd coming toward him. He said to Philip,

PHILIP -- WHERE CAN WE BUY FOOD FOR THESE PEOPLE?

FOR **ALL** OF THEM? WHY, THERE MUST BE 5,000 MEN -- BESIDES THE WOMEN AND CHILDREN.

"Where can we buy bread for all these people to eat?" ⁶(Jesus asked Philip this question to test him. Jesus already knew what he planned to do.)

⁷Philip answered, "We would all have to work a month to buy enough bread for each person here to have only a little piece."

⁸Another follower there was Andrew. He was Simon Peter's brother. Andrew said, ⁹"Here is a boy with five loaves of barley bread and two little fish. But that is not enough for so many people."

¹⁰Jesus said, "Tell the people to sit down." This was a very grassy place. There were about 5,000 men who sat down there. ¹¹Then Jesus took the loaves of bread. He thanked God for the bread and gave it to the people who were sitting there. He did the same with the fish. He gave them as much as they wanted.

¹²They all had enough to eat. When they had finished, Jesus said to his followers, "Gather the pieces of fish and bread that were not eaten. Don't waste anything." ¹³So they gathered up the pieces that were left. They filled 12 large baskets with the pieces that were left of the five barley loaves.

From John 6

More⫸

? When the young boy offered his lunch to Jesus, do you think he expected it to feed 5,000 men (not to mention the women and children)? Why?

? What did Jesus do with the small lunch?

? Sometimes a situation seems impossible. But when we ask for God's help, He will give us ideas for ways to solve the problem. Think about a situation where you want to have more free time but you still have to do homework and chores around the house. Name two ways that will help you to organize your work so that you'll get it done faster.

Our Lord is great and very powerful. There is no limit to what he knows.
Psalm 147:5

Thanks, God, for giving me the abilities and talents to think up ways to get things done. Help me to remember that You are always there to give me new ideas when I face a problem. Amen.

LOOK! EVERYONE HERE IS GETTING ALL THE FOOD HE WANTS.

IT'S A MIRACLE!

GATHER UP THE FOOD THAT REMAINS.

RESOURCEFUL PERSON DEVISES WAYS AND MEANS TO GET A JOB ACCOMPLISHED. THINK ABOUT YOUR BEDROOM (WHOA! LET'S NOT!). WRITE DOWN A THREE-STEP PLAN TO EVACUATE THE MESS AND MAKE YOUR MOM HAPPY. CONSIDER WHAT WOULD BE THE MOST TIME-EFFICIENT WAY SO THAT YOU CAN QUICKLY GET TO MORE IMPORTANT ISSUES--PLAYING BASEBALL, RIDING YOUR BIKE, ETC.

PROJECT: MESS EVACUATION
MY PLAN IS TO:

1.

2.

3.

TIME TAKEN TO ACCOMPLISH THE JOB:

SIGNED,

_____ ,

A VERY RESOURCEFUL PERSON

115

WALKING ON WATER

HOW MUCH FARTHER TO LAND?

WE'RE ONLY HALF WAY.

THEN Jesus made his followers get into the boat. He told them to go ahead of him to the other side of the lake. Jesus stayed there to tell the people they could go home. 23After he said good-bye to them, he went alone up into the hills to pray. It was late, and Jesus was there alone. 24By this time, the boat was already far away on the lake. The boat was having trouble because of the waves, and the wind was blowing against it.

25Between three and six o'clock in the morning, Jesus' followers were still in the boat. Jesus came to them. He was walking on the water. 26When the followers saw him walking on the water, they were afraid. They said, "It's a ghost!" and cried out in fear.

27But Jesus quickly spoke to them. He said, "Have courage! It is I! Don't be afraid."

28Peter said, "Lord, if that is really you, then tell me to come to you on the water."

29Jesus said, "Come."

And Peter left the boat and walked on the water to Jesus. 30But when Peter saw the wind and the waves, he became afraid and began to sink. He shouted, "Lord, save me!"

31Then Jesus reached out his hand and caught Peter. Jesus said, "Your faith is small. Why did you doubt?"

32After Peter and Jesus were in the boat, the wind became calm. 33Then those who were in the boat worshiped Jesus and said, "Truly you are the Son of God!"

From Matthew 14

INSTANTLY PETER JUMPS FROM THE BOAT AND STARTS WALKING TOWARD JESUS. BUT WHEN HE SEES THE POWER OF THE WIND, HE LOSES FAITH-- AND BEGINS TO SINK...

? What did Peter say to Jesus when he knew the image on the water was not a ghost?

? What did Peter do when Jesus told him to come?

? It took a lot of courage for Peter to get out of the boat. He had to trust that Jesus would take care of him. Think of an example in your life–maybe someone was in an accident or really sick or maybe your dad lost his job–where you had to have courage and just keep believing that God would take care of the situation. How did you feel? Were you a little scared?

Lord, thank You for being there when I need You. Help me to keep my eyes on You and not on my problems. Give me courage and make me strong. Amen.

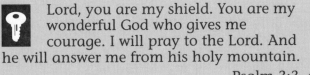

Lord, you are my shield. You are my wonderful God who gives me courage. I will pray to the Lord. And he will answer me from his holy mountain.

Psalm 3:3, 4

More‖‖➡

AS LONG AS PETER LOOKED AT JESUS, HE HAD COURAGE. WHEN HE STARTED LOOKING AT THE WIND AND THE WAVES, HE STARTED TO SINK. DRAW A PICTURE OF YOURSELF FULL OF COURAGE. THE NEXT TIME YOU FEEL DOWN AND NEED ENCOURAGEMENT, TURN TO THIS PAGE AND REMIND YOURSELF THAT GOD IS IN CONTROL.

Initiative

THEN a teacher of the law stood up.

He was trying to test Jesus. He said, "Teacher, what must I do to get life forever?"

26Jesus said to him, "What is written in the law? What do you read there?"

27The man answered, "Love the Lord your God. Love him with all your heart, all your soul, all your strength, and all your mind." Also, "You must love your neighbor as you love yourself."

28Jesus said to him, "Your answer is right. Do this and you will have life forever."

29But the man wanted to show that the way he was living was right. So he said to Jesus, "And who is my neighbor?"

30To answer this question, Jesus said, "A man was going down the road from Jerusalem to Jericho. Some robbers attacked him. They tore off his clothes and beat him. Then they left him lying there, almost dead.

A Samaritan Comes to the Rescue

31It happened that a Jewish priest was going down that road. When the priest saw the man, he walked by on the other side of the road. 32Next, a Levite came there. He went over and looked at the man. Then he walked by on the other side of the road. 33Then a Samaritan traveling down the road came to where the hurt man was lying. He saw the man and felt very sorry for him. 34The Samaritan went to him and poured olive oil and wine on his wounds and bandaged them. He put the hurt man on his own donkey and took him to an inn. At the inn, the Samaritan took care of him. 35The next day, the Samaritan brought out two silver coins and gave them to the innkeeper. The Samaritan said, "Take care of this man. If you spend more money on him, I will pay it back to you when I come again.' "

36Then Jesus said, "Which one of these three men do you think was a neighbor to the man who was attacked by the robbers?"

37The teacher of the law answered, "The one who helped him."

Jesus said to him, "Then go and do the same thing he did!"

From Luke 10

More!⏩

119

NOW I SEE -- MY NEIGHBOR IS ANYONE WHO NEEDS ME.

? Neither the priest nor the Levite (temple worker) stopped to help the injured man. Why do you think they didn't stop?

? The Samaritan bandaged the hurt man's wounds. What else did he do to help the man?

? The Samaritan saw the man's need and immediately took action to help him. If you saw an injured person lying in the street today, what might you do to help him?

Remember the Lord in everything you do. And he will give you success.

Proverbs 3:6

Lord, show me ways that I can help others. Then help me take action to do what You want me to do. Thanks, Lord. Amen.

A PERSON WITH INITIATIVE SEES A PROBLEM AND THEN TAKES ACTION TO RESOLVE THAT PROBLEM. THINK OF SOMEONE IN YOUR CLASS AT SCHOOL OR CHURCH WHO NEEDS A FRIEND. WRITE DOWN AN ACTION PLAN OF HOW YOU CAN HELP THAT PERSON FEEL SPECIAL.

ACTION PLAN

PERSON WHO NEEDS A FRIEND: _____

THINGS I CAN DO TO HELP THAT PERSON:

1. _____

2. _____

3. _____

DATE I WILL PUT THIS PLAN INTO ACTION: _____

SIGNED _____, CIO

(CHIEF INITIATING OFFICER)

The Son who Left Home

THEN Jesus said, "A man had two sons. [12]The younger son said to his father, 'Give me my share of the property.' So the father divided the property between his two sons. [13]Then the younger son gathered up all that was his and left. He traveled far away to another country. There he wasted his money in foolish living. [14]He spent everything that he had. Soon after that, the land became very dry, and there was no rain. There was not enough food to eat anywhere in the country. The son was hungry and needed money. [15]So he got a job with one of the citizens there. The man sent the son into the fields to feed pigs. [16]The son was so hungry that he was willing to eat the food the pigs were eating. But no one gave him anything. [17]The son realized that he had been very foolish. He thought, 'All of my father's servants have plenty of food. But I am here, almost dying with hunger. [18]I will leave and return to my father. I'll say to him: Father, I have sinned against God and have done wrong to you. [19]I am not good enough to be called your son. But let me be like one of your servants.' [20]So the son left and went to his father.

"While the son was still a long way off, his father saw him coming. He felt sorry for his son. So the father ran to him, and hugged and kissed him. [21]The son said, 'Father, I have sinned against God and have done wrong to you. I am not good enough to be called your son.' [22]But the father said to his servants, 'Hurry! Bring the best clothes and put them on him. Also, put a ring on his finger and sandals on his feet. [23]And get our fat calf and kill it. Then we can have a feast and celebrate! [24]My son was dead, but now he is alive again! He was lost, but now he is found!' So they began to celebrate.

More!

From Luke 15

FATHER, I WANT TO RUN MY OWN LIFE. PLEASE GIVE ME THE SHARE OF YOUR MONEY THAT WILL SOMEDAY BE MINE.

I HAD HOPED YOU WOULD STAY HOME AND HELP WITH THE WORK HERE-- BUT IF YOU WANT THE MONEY, YOU MAY HAVE IT.

THE YOUNG MAN GOES TO ANOTHER COUNTRY-- WHERE HE SPENDS HIS MONEY EATING AND DRINKING WITH BAD COMPANIONS. AT LAST HIS MONEY IS GONE--AND THE ONLY JOB HE CAN GET IS CARING FOR A FARMER'S PIGS.

MY FATHER'S SERVANTS LIVE BETTER THAN THIS! I'M GOING HOME AND ASK MY FATHER TO LET ME WORK FOR HIM--NOT AS HIS SON, BUT AS A SERVANT!

? The younger son made some bad choices. What were they?

? When he made the wise choice to return to his father's house, how did his father react toward him?

? All of us make good and bad choices. Think of an example of a good choice that you made this past week. What might have happened if you had chosen differently?

Lord, help me to make wise choices. Help me not to act first and think later. Lead me to make the best choice the first time. Amen.

The Lord says, "I will make you wise. I will show you where to go. I will guide you and watch over you."

Psalm 32:8

FATHER! I HAVE SINNED AGAINST HEAVEN AND YOU. I'M NO LONGER WORTHY TO BE CALLED YOUR SON.

WE SHOULD GET WISER AS WE GROW OLDER BECAUSE WE CAN LEARN FROM OUR EXPERIENCES. IF YOU ASKED THE SON IF HE'D HAVE DONE THE SAME THING OVER A SECOND TIME, HE MIGHT HAVE SAID, "NO WAY! I'LL ONLY MAKE THAT MISTAKE ONCE!" THINK OF TWO QUESTIONS YOU HAVE ABOUT A PROBLEM IN YOUR LIFE, PERHAPS WITH A FRIEND OR A FAMILY MEMBER. THEN TALK TO SOMEONE OLDER--A PARENT, TEACHER, OR PASTOR--AND ASK FOR ADVICE. ASK THIS PERSON TO PRAY WITH YOU AND THEN WRITE THE WORDS OF ADVICE HERE.

The Sad Rich Man

A **Jewish leader asked Jesus, "Good Teacher,** what must I do to get the life that continues forever?"

¹⁹Jesus said to him, "Why do you call me good? Only God is good. ²⁰You know the commands: 'You must not be guilty of adultery. You must not murder anyone. You must not steal. You must not tell lies about your neighbor in court. Honor your father and mother.'"

²¹But the leader said, "I have obeyed all these commands since I was a boy!"

²²When Jesus heard this, he said to him, "But there is still one more thing you need to do. Sell everything you have and give the money to the poor. You will have a reward in heaven. Then come and follow me!" ²³But when the man heard this, he became very sad because he was very rich.

²⁴When Jesus saw that the man was sad, he said, "It will be very hard for rich people to enter the kingdom of God! ²⁵It would be easier for a camel to go through the eye of a needle than for a rich person to enter the kingdom of God!"

From Luke 18

124

BUT I HAVE KEPT THE LAWS -- SINCE I WAS A BOY.

YOU NEED TO DO ONE THING MORE -- SELL ALL THAT YOU HAVE, GIVE THE MONEY TO THE POOR, AND FOLLOW ME.

? Did the man consider himself to be a good man? Why?

? What was the one thing that the man didn't want to do?

? Some people want to give only a part of their life to God. They don't want to make a total commitment. They say, "I'll give you this much, God, but not my WHOLE life." How do you think God feels about this kind of commitment?

... The Lord is our God. He is the only Lord. Love the Lord your God with all your heart, soul and strength.

Deuteronomy 6:4, 5

Thanks, God, for loving me. Help me to commit my whole life to You and be willing to do whatever You ask me to do. Amen.

Morell**⫸**

THINK ABOUT YOUR COMMITMENT TO GOD. DO YOU WANT TO LEARN ABOUT HIM? . . . DO THINGS FOR HIM? . . . LIVE BY HIS RULES AND PROMISES? WRITE A NOTE TO GOD ABOUT HOW YOU FEEL.

DEAR GOD:

JESUS was going through the city of Jericho.

2In Jericho there was a man named Zacchaeus. He was a wealthy, very important tax collector. 3He wanted to see who Jesus was, but he was too short to see above the crowd. 4He ran ahead to a place where he knew Jesus would come. He climbed a sycamore tree so he could see Jesus. 5When Jesus came to that place, he looked up and saw Zacchaeus in the tree. He said to him, "Zacchaeus, hurry and come down! I must stay at your house today."

6Zacchaeus came down quickly. He was pleased to have Jesus in his house. 7All the people saw this and began to complain, "Look at the kind of man Jesus stays with. Zacchaeus is a sinner!"

8But Zacchaeus said to the Lord, "I will give half of my money to the poor. If I have cheated anyone, I will pay that person back four times more!"

9Jesus said, "Salvation has come to this house today. This man truly belongs to the family of Abraham. 10The Son of Man came to find lost people and save them."

From Luke 19

? What was Zacchaeus's job?

? What did Zacchaeus say that would let you know that he didn't want to cheat people anymore?

? Being a good steward (or manager) of your money is important to God. He wants you to use money wisely and be honest in your dealings with other people. Think of some wise ways that money can be used to get God's work done. Some examples might be to help missionaries, to support the minister, to buy needed items for the church, etc.

"Give, and you will receive. . . . The way you give to others is the way God will give to you."

Luke 6:38

Lord, help me to be a good manager of my time, talents, and money. Remind me that You come first in my life and that I should always give You the best of what I have to give. Amen.

GOD WANTS US TO BE GOOD STEWARDS OR MANAGERS OF ALL OUR RESOURCES: OUR TIME, OUR TALENTS AND ABILITIES, AND OUR MONEY. WRITE ONE THING YOU COULD GIVE TO GOD IN EACH OF THESE AREAS. FOR EXAMPLE,

TIME: SATURDAY MORNING . . . 2 HOURS

TALENT: MOWING MRS. JONES'S LAWN

MONEY: EARN TEN DOLLARS FROM JOB TO GIVE IN MISSIONS' OFFERING ON SUNDAY.

YOUR EXAMPLE:
TIME:
TALENT:
MONEY:

128

Wash My Stinky Feet? No Way!

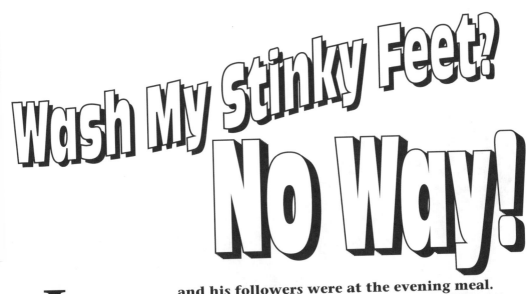

JESUS **and his followers were at the evening meal.** [4]During the meal Jesus stood up and took off his outer clothing. Taking a towel, he wrapped it around his waist. [5]Then he poured water into a bowl and began to wash the followers' feet. He dried them with the towel that was wrapped around him.

[6]Jesus came to Simon Peter. But Peter said to Jesus, "Lord, are you going to wash my feet?"

[7]Jesus answered, "You don't understand what I am doing now. But you will understand later."

[8]Peter said, "No! You will never wash my feet."

Jesus answered, "If I don't wash your feet, then you are not one of my people."

[9]Simon Peter answered, "Lord, after you wash my feet, wash my hands and my head, too!"

[10]Jesus said, "After a person has had a bath, his whole body is clean. He needs only to wash his feet. And you men are clean, but not all of you." [11]Jesus knew who would turn against him. That is why Jesus said, "Not all of you are clean."

[12]When he had finished washing their feet, he put on his clothes and sat down again. Jesus asked, "Do you understand what I have just done for you? [13]You call me 'Teacher' and 'Lord.' And this is right, because that is what I am. [14]I, your Lord and Teacher, have washed your feet. So you also should wash each other's feet. [15]I did this as an example for you. So you should do as I have done for you. [16]I tell you the truth. A servant is not greater than his master. A messenger is not greater than the one who sent him. [17]If you know these things, you will be happy if you do them.

PETER AND JOHN PREPARE FOR THE FEAST, AND THAT EVENING JESUS JOINS THE TWELVE IN THE UPPER ROOM. AFTER THEY ARE SEATED JESUS KNEELS, LIKE A SERVANT, TO WASH THE FEET OF HIS DISCIPLES.

NO, LORD. I'M NOT GOOD ENOUGH TO HAVE **YOU** WAIT ON ME!

From John 13   Morell⟶ 129

? Why did Jesus wash His follower's feet?

? What did Jesus say that would give us a clue as to how we should treat each other?

? Washing stinky feet is not a job that Jesus had to do. Yet He did this to show us what humility is. Think of a dirty job that you've had to do. How did you feel while you were doing it? Did you feel like a king or company president when you were through?

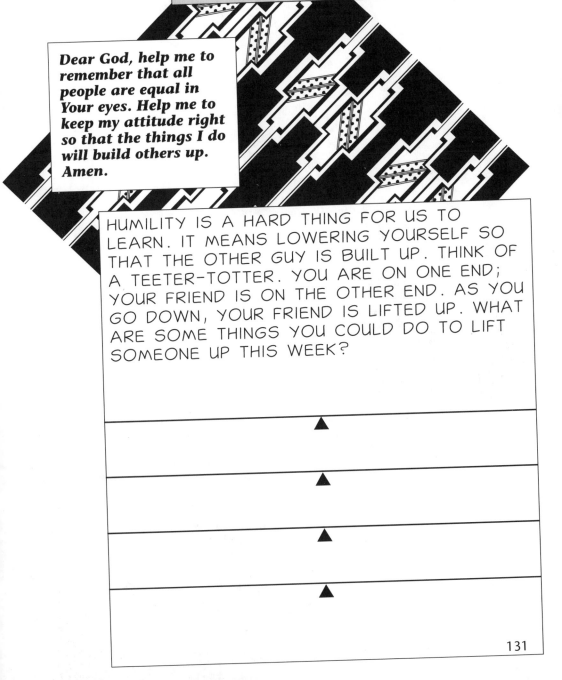

When you do things, do not let selfishness or pride be your guide. Be humble and give more honor to others than to yourselves.

Philippians 2:3

Dear God, help me to remember that all people are equal in Your eyes. Help me to keep my attitude right so that the things I do will build others up. Amen.

HUMILITY IS A HARD THING FOR US TO LEARN. IT MEANS LOWERING YOURSELF SO THAT THE OTHER GUY IS BUILT UP. THINK OF A TEETER-TOTTER. YOU ARE ON ONE END; YOUR FRIEND IS ON THE OTHER END. AS YOU GO DOWN, YOUR FRIEND IS LIFTED UP. WHAT ARE SOME THINGS YOU COULD DO TO LIFT SOMEONE UP THIS WEEK?

131

Asleep on the Job

QUIETLY, THEY LEAVE THE UPPER ROOM. THEY WALK THROUGH THE MOONLIT STREETS OF THE CITY, OUT AN EAST GATE, AND ACROSS A VALLEY TO THE GARDEN OF GETHSEMANE ON THE MOUNT OF OLIVES.

THEN **Jesus went with his followers to a place called Gethsemane.** He said to them, "Sit here while I go over there and pray." [37]He told Peter and the two sons of Zebedee to come with him. Then Jesus began to be very sad and troubled. [38]He said to Peter and the two sons of Zebedee, "My heart is full of sorrow and breaking with sadness. Stay here with me and watch."

[39]Then Jesus walked a little farther away from them. He fell to the ground and prayed, "My Father, if it is possible, do not give me this cup of suffering. But do what you want, not what I want." [40]Then Jesus went back to his followers and found them asleep. Jesus said to Peter, "You men could not stay awake with me for one hour? [41]Stay awake and pray for strength against temptation. Your spirit wants to do what is right. But your body is weak."

[42]Then Jesus went away a second time. He prayed, "My Father, if it is not possible for this painful thing to be taken from me, and if I must do it, then I pray that what you want will be done."

[43]Then Jesus went back to the followers. Again he found them asleep, because their eyes were heavy. [44]So Jesus left them and went away one more time and prayed. This third time he prayed, he said the same thing.

[45]Then Jesus went back to the followers and said, "You are still sleeping and resting? The time has come for the Son of Man to be given to sinful people. [46]Get up. We must go.

From Matthew 26

AT THE ENTRANCE JESUS ASKS EIGHT OF THE DISCIPLES WHILE HE TAKES HIS CLOSEST DISCIPLES, PETER, JAMES, JOHN FARTHER INTO THE GARDEN.

THIS IS A SAD NIGHT FOR ME -- STAY HERE AND WATCH WHILE I GO ALONE TO PRAY.

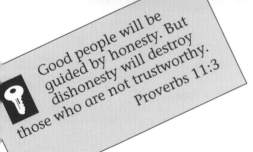

Good people will be guided by honesty. But dishonesty will destroy those who are not trustworthy. Proverbs 11:3

Lord, help me to be a trustworthy person. Remind me to keep the promises I make to others. Amen.

? What did Jesus tell Peter and the sons of Zebedee the first time He went to pray?

? What did Jesus find every time He came back from prayer? Could He trust them to stay awake and pray? Why?

? Being trustworthy means that you are dependable and others can count on you. When you say you'll do something, it will get done. Can people count on you to do what you promise to do? Give an example of when you kept a promise to do something for someone.

More

PEOPLE LEARN TO TRUST YOU WHEN YOU CARRY OUT YOUR PROMISES. BY FOLLOWING THROUGH, YOU PROVE TO OTHERS THAT YOU ARE TRUSTWORTHY. WRITE A COUPON TO YOUR MOM OR DAD PROMISING TO DO ONE JOB BY A CERTAIN DATE. THEN COPY YOUR COUPON ON ANOTHER PIECE OF PAPER. PLACE THE COPIED COUPON BY HIS OR HER PLATE AT THE NEXT MEAL. (YOU MIGHT WANT TO ROLL IT UP AND PUT A SMALL RIBBON AROUND IT.)

JOB COUPON

TO:

JOB TO BE DONE:

COMPLETED BY

SIGNED:

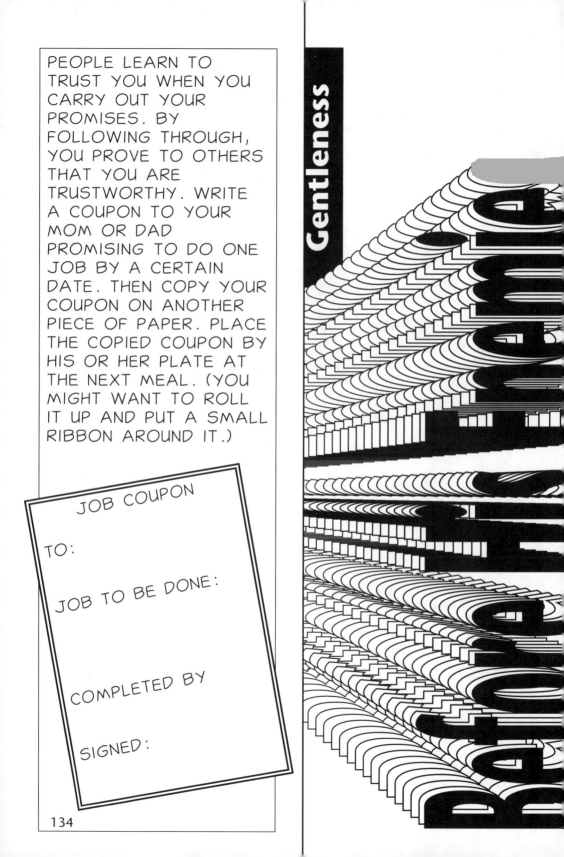

Gentleness

THEN Jesus said to the crowd, "You came to get me with swords and clubs as if I were a criminal.

Every day I sat in the Temple teaching. You did not arrest me there. 56But all these things have happened so that it will be as the prophets wrote." Then all of Jesus' followers left him and ran away.

57Those men who arrested Jesus led him to the house of Caiaphas, the high priest. The teachers of the law and the older Jewish leaders were gathered there. 58Peter followed Jesus but did not go near him. He followed Jesus to the courtyard of the high priest's house. He sat down with the guards to see what would happen to Jesus.

59The leading priests and the Jewish council tried to find something false against Jesus so that they could kill him. 60Many people

came and told lies about him. But the council could find no real reason to kill Jesus. Then two people came and said, 61"This man said, 'I can destroy the Temple of God and build it again in three days.' "

62Then the high priest stood up and said to Jesus, "Aren't you going to answer? Don't you have something to say about their charges against you?" 63But Jesus said nothing.

Again the high priest said to Jesus, "You must swear to this. I command you by the power of the living God to tell us the truth. Tell us, are you the Christ, the Son of God?"

64Jesus answered, "Yes, I am. But I tell you, in the future you will see the Son of Man sitting at the right hand of God, the Powerful One. And you will see him coming in clouds in the sky."

65When the high priest heard this, he was very angry. He tore his clothes and said, "This man has said things that are against God! We don't need any more witnesses. You all heard him say these things against God. 66What do you think?"

The people answered, "He is guilty, and he must die."

67Then the people there spit in Jesus' face and beat him with their fists. Others slapped Jesus. 68They said, "Prove to us that you are a prophet, you Christ! Tell us who hit you!"

From Matthew 26

Morell▶

135

Following his arrest, Jesus is brought to the palace of the high priest. False witnesses boldly accuse him of many things -- but they can prove nothing. Finally the high priest questions the prisoner.

ARE YOU THE CHRIST, THE SON OF GOD?

I AM.

Lord, help me to be more gentle to others. Remind me that when I fail, You are always gentle to me. Amen.

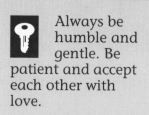

Always be humble and gentle. Be patient and accept each other with love.

Ephesians 4:2

? How did the people act toward Jesus?

? Did Jesus have the power to kill the leaders and the people if He had wanted to? How do you know?

? Being gentle means that you have the power to take control, to show force or anger, but you choose not to. What can happen when we lose our temper and get angry?

USUALLY WE ARE NOT GENTLE. WE YELL AND DEMAND OUR OWN WAY. WE THINK IF WE ACT TOUGH, WE'LL ACCOMPLISH WHAT WE WANT. THINK OF A SITUATION WHERE YOU COULD GIVE A GENTLE ANSWER INSTEAD OF DEMANDING YOUR OWN WAY. FOR EXAMPLE, INSTEAD OF YELLING AT A BROTHER OR SISTER, YOU RESPOND WITH GENTLENESS. WHAT DO YOU THINK WILL HAPPEN?

(TRY THIS NEXT TIME YOU GET INTO A FIGHT. WRITE DOWN WHAT ACTUALLY HAPPENED WHEN YOU TRIED THE GENTLE METHOD.)

"I Never Saw Him Before"

PETER, BEFORE THE COCK CROWS YOU WILL DENY ME THREE TIMES.

DENY MY LORD? NEVER! MY SWORD IS READY THIS MINUTE FOR THE FIRST PERSON WHO TRIES TO HARM HIM.

AT **that time, Peter was sitting in the courtyard.** A servant girl came to him and said, "You were with Jesus, that man from Galilee."

70But Peter said that he was never with Jesus. He said this to all the people there. Peter said, "I don't know what you are talking about."

71Then he left the courtyard. At the gate, another girl saw him. She said to the people there, "This man was with Jesus of Nazareth."

72Again, Peter said that he was never with Jesus. Peter said, "I swear that I don't know this man Jesus!"

73A short time later, some people standing there went to Peter. They said, "We know you are one of those men who followed Jesus. We know this because of the way you talk."

74Then Peter began to curse. He said, "May a curse fall on me if I'm not telling the truth. I don't know the man." After Peter said this, a rooster crowed. 75Then he remembered what Jesus had told him: "Before the rooster crows, you will say three times that you don't know me." Then Peter went outside and cried painfully.

From Matthew 26

More⏵

138

? What did Jesus tell Peter he would do before the rooster crowed?

? How did Peter feel after he heard the rooster?

? A faithful friend is one who is always there — in good times or bad. Peter was not a faithful friend. When the going got rough, he got scared and denied he even knew Jesus. Have you ever had someone who you thought was a friend go against you? How did it make you feel?

Dear God, thank You for being a faithful friend to me. Show me ways that I can be a good friend to others. Amen.

Some friends may ruin you. But a real friend will be more loyal than a brother.
Proverbs 18:24

DO YOU HAVE A FAITHFUL FRIEND--
SOMEONE WHO IS THERE IN GOOD TIMES OR
BAD? WRITE DOWN THREE THINGS THAT YOU
LIKE ABOUT THAT PERSON. THEN THINK OF
THREE THINGS YOU COULD DO TO SHOW THAT
YOU ARE A FAITHFUL FRIEND TO YOUR FRIEND
(LISTEN WHEN HE OR SHE NEEDS TO TALK,
EAT LUNCH TOGETHER, ETC.).

MY FRIEND'S NAME IS: _____
I LIKE MY FRIEND BECAUSE:

1. _____

2. _____

3. _____

SOME WAYS THAT I CAN SHOW THAT I AM A
FAITHFUL FRIEND ARE:

1. _____

2. _____

3. _____

Between 2 Criminal

THERE **were also two criminals led out with Jesus to be killed.** 33Jesus and the two criminals were taken to a place called the Skull. There the soldiers nailed Jesus to his cross. They also nailed the criminals to their crosses, one beside Jesus on the right and the other beside Jesus on the left. . . . 39One of the criminals began to shout insults at Jesus: "Aren't you the Christ? Then save yourself! And save us too!"

40But the other criminal stopped him. He said, "You should fear God! You are getting the same punishment as he is. 41We are punished justly; we should die. But this man has done nothing wrong!" 42Then this criminal said to Jesus, "Jesus, remember me when you come into your kingdom!"

43Then Jesus said to him, "Listen! What I say is true: Today you will be with me in paradise!"

From Luke 23

FATHER, FORGIVE THEM: FOR THEY KNOW NOT WHAT THEY DO.

> A good person speaks with wisdom. He says what is fair.
>
> Psalm 37:30

God, help me treat others fairly. Remind me to say kind words and keep a good attitude when things I face seem unfair. Amen.

? What happened to Jesus and the two criminals when they were taken to the place called the Skull?

? What did one of the criminals say to let you know that he realized something wasn't fair about Jesus' punishment?

? Some things around us don't seem fair—why do good people lose their jobs or get cancer or get hit by a car? We can look at our everyday life and wonder why some people always get the special parts in plays, get to be team captain, or have so many friends. If we try, we can find unfair things all around us. Name other things that you think are unfair.

SOME THINGS IN LIFE ARE UNFAIR. WHAT MATTERS TO GOD IS HOW YOU HANDLE UNFAIR SITUATIONS. BY CHECKING WITH GOD'S WORD YOU CAN DISCOVER SOME HELPFUL KEYS TO HELP KEEP YOUR ATTITUDE ON TRACK. LOOK UP THESE SCRIPTURES. THEN WRITE A SHORT DESCRIPTION OF WHAT THE VERSE SAYS TO YOU ABOUT FAIRNESS.

☆ ACTS 10:34--TO GOD EVERYONE IS THE SAME

☆ ROMANS 12:10--

☆ PROVERBS 21:3--

☆ HEBREWS 13:16--

☆ PROVERBS 21:15--

TRULY THIS MAN WAS GOD'S SON!

SO LOVED THE WORLD FOR GOD

FATHER, INTO THY HANDS I COMMIT MY SPIRIT.

IT **was about noon, and the whole land became dark** until three o'clock in the afternoon. 45There was no sun! The curtain in the Temple was torn into two pieces. 46Jesus cried out in a loud voice, "Father, I give you my life." After Jesus said this, he died. 47The army officer there saw what happened. He praised God, saying, "I know this was a good man!" 48Many people had gathered there to watch this thing. When they saw what happened, they returned home. They beat their chests because they were so sad.

From Luke 23

? What was unusual about what happened when Jesus died?

? How did the army officer, Jesus' followers, and the other people who were watching act when Jesus died?

? It's hard for us to understand how Jesus could take all the sins of every person who has ever lived and then die to pay for those sins with His blood. Sin could only be blotted out by sacrificing a lamb. Jesus became a lamb and gave His blood for us. What might have happened if Jesus would have decided He didn't want to die on the cross?

More

You are God's children whom he loves. So try to be like God. Live a life of love. Love other people just as Christ loved us. Christ gave himself for us—he was a sweet-smelling offering and sacrifice to God.

Ephesians 5:1, 2

Jesus, thank You for going to the cross to pay for my sin. Thank You for loving me. Help me to think of different ways to show You how much I love You. Amen.

GOD LOVED US SO MUCH THAT HE GAVE HIS ONLY SON SO THAT WE CAN HAVE ETERNAL LIFE WITH HIM IN HEAVEN. DRAW A PICTURE THAT SHOWS YOUR LOVE FOR GOD. YOU MIGHT LIKE TO MAKE A VALENTINE TO GOD.

A Job for Peter

Peter Peter Peter Peter Peter

PETER IS SO EAGER TO REACH JESUS THAT HE JUMPS INTO THE WATER AND SWIMS TO LAND. THE OTHERS BRING THE BOAT IN AND ANCHOR IT OFFSHORE. AFTER THE NET IS PULLED IN, JESUS CALLS TO HIS HUNGRY DISCIPLES.

COME AND EAT.

LATER, Jesus showed himself to his **followers** by Lake Galilee. This is how it happened: . . .
³Simon Peter said, "I am going out to fish."

The other followers said, "We will go with you." So they went out and got into the boat. They fished that night but caught nothing.

⁴Early the next morning Jesus stood on the shore. But the followers did not know that it was Jesus. ⁵Then he said to them, "Friends, have you caught any fish?"

They answered, "No."

⁶He said, "Throw your net into the water on the right side of the boat, and you will find some." So they did this. They caught so many fish that they could not pull the net back into the boat.

⁷The follower whom Jesus loved said to Peter, "It is the Lord!" When Peter heard him say this, he wrapped his coat around himself. (Peter had taken his clothes off.) Then he jumped into the water. ⁸The other followers went to shore in the boat, dragging the net full of fish.

From John 21

Morel◄►

They were not very far from shore, only about 100 yards. 9When the followers stepped out of the boat and onto the shore, they saw a fire of hot coals. There were fish on the fire, and there was bread.

10Then Jesus said, "Bring some of the fish that you caught."

11Simon Peter went into the boat and pulled the net to the shore. It was full of big fish. There were 153. Even though there were so many, the net did not tear. 12Jesus said to them, "Come and eat." None of the followers dared ask him, "Who are you?" They knew it was the Lord. 13Jesus came and took the bread and gave it to them. He also gave them the fish . . . .

15When they finished eating, Jesus said to Simon Peter, "Simon son of John do you love me more than these?"

He answered, "Yes, Lord, you know that I love you."

Jesus said, "Take care of my lambs."

16Again Jesus said, "Simon son of John do you love me?"

He answered, "Yes, Lord, you know that I love you."

Jesus said, "Take care of my sheep."

17A third time he said, "Simon son of John do you love me?"

Peter was hurt because Jesus asked him the third time, "Do you love me?" Peter said, "Lord, you know everything. You know that I love you!"

He said to him, "Take care of my sheep."

? How many fish did they catch after following Jesus' suggestion? Why do you think Jesus told them to cast their net on the other side of the boat?

? How many times did Jesus ask Peter the question, "Do you love Me?"

? Jesus may have been testing Peter's loyalty by asking him the same question so many times. Sometimes it's easy to give a quick answer and not think about what we are saying. If a friend asked you, "Are you really my friend?", what would that question mean to you? Does it mean more than just saying "Hi!" at school?

He guards those who are fair to others. He protects those who are loyal to him.

Proverbs 2:8

Dear God, thank You for showing Your love to me every day. Help me to show loyalty to You by trying to do things that please You. Give me more ideas through Your Word on how I can do this. Thanks. Amen.

JESUS WANTED PETER TO GO BEYOND SAYING THAT HE LOVED JESUS. HE WANTED PETER TO PROVE HIS LOYALTY WITH ACTION--TAKE CARE OF HIS SHEEP (OR HIS FOLLOWERS). JESUS WANTS MORE THAN AN "I LOVE YOU" FROM YOU. HE WANTS YOU TO TAKE ACTION TO SHOW YOUR LOYALTY TO HIM. NAME SOME WAYS THAT YOU CAN SHOW YOUR LOVE AND LOYALTY TO THE LORD.

1 _____

2 _____

3 _____

4 _____

5 _____

6 _____

It's Hard to Wait

AFTER his death, [Jesus] **showed himself** to them and . . . spoke to them about the Kingdom of God. . . . ⁴He said, "The Father has made you a promise . . . . Wait here to receive this promise. . . . The Holy Spirit will come to you. Then you will receive power. You will be my witnesses—in Jerusalem, in all of Judea, in Samaria, and in every part of the world."

Chapter 2 When the day of Pentecost came, they were all together in one place. ²Suddenly a noise came from heaven. It sounded like a strong wind blowing. This noise filled the whole house where they were sitting. . . . ⁴They were all filled with the Holy Spirit, and they began to speak different languages. The Holy Spirit was giving them the power to speak these languages.

⁵There were some religious Jews staying in Jerusalem who were from every country in the world.

³⁸Peter said to them, "Change your hearts and lives and be baptized, each one of you, in the name of Jesus Christ for the forgiveness of your sins. And you will receive the gift of the Holy Spirit. ³⁹This promise is for you. It is also for your children and for all who are far away. It is for everyone the Lord our God calls to himself."

From Acts 1, 2

THE ANGELS DISAPPEAR, AND PETER TURNS TO THE OTHERS.

LET'S DO WHAT JESUS TOLD US TO DO--GO BACK TO JERUSALEM AND WAIT FOR THE POWER HE PROMISED TO SEND US BEFORE WE BEGIN HIS WORK.

SO THE DISCIPLES, WHO HAD ONCE FLED FOR FEAR OF BEING ARRESTED AS FRIENDS OF JESUS, RETURN TO THE CITY--KNOWING THAT JESUS IS DEPENDING ON THEM TO CARRY ON THE WORK FOR WHICH HE WAS CRUCIFIED.

? What were Jesus' followers waiting for?

? What would this promise enable them to do?

? Whether we know what's in the future or not, waiting is the hardest part. Think of a time that you had to wait for a long time to receive something special.

My brothers, you will have many kinds of troubles. But when these things happen, you should be very happy. . . . This will give you patience.

James 1:2, 3

Lord, help me to learn patience so that I can speak and act in a way that will always please You. Thanks. Amen.

Morell ▶

SOMETIMES GOD USES WAITING TO HELP US LEARN PATIENCE. PATIENCE IS THE ABILITY TO GO THROUGH PROBLEMS WITH A CALM ATTITUDE, WITHOUT COMPLAINING. IT ALLOWS US THE TIME TO HEAR THE OTHER SIDE OF THE STORY BEFORE SAYING ANGRY WORDS WE WILL REGRET. WRITE GOD A NOTE AND TELL HIM ABOUT ONE PROBLEM YOU'RE HAVING TROUBLE WORKING OUT. ASK HIM FOR PATIENCE TO SOLVE THE PROBLEM HIS WAY.

DEAR GOD:

ON THE FIRST DAY OF THE NEW TESTAMENT CHURCH, 3,000 PEOPLE WERE ADDED TO THE NUMBER OF BELIEVERS IN JESUS CHRIST. NEW BELIEVERS WERE EVERYWHERE, ALL HAVING A GREAT TIME. . . .

WHEN PETER BOLDLY TELLS THE PEOPLE IN JERUSALEM THAT THEY CONDEMNED GOD'S CHOSEN ONE TO DIE, THEY ASK, "WHAT CAN WE DO?" "REPENT AND BE BAPTIZED IN THE NAME OF THE ONE YOU CRUCIFIED," PETER REPLIES. ONE BY ONE THE PEOPLE CRY OUT...

O GOD, FORGIVE MY SINS, IN THE NAME OF YOUR SON, JESUS CHRIST, WHO CAME TO SAVE ME!

THEY **spent their time learning the apostles' teaching.** And they continued to share, to break bread, and to pray together.

⁴³The apostles were doing many miracles and signs. And everyone felt great respect for God. ⁴⁴All the believers stayed together. They shared everything. ⁴⁵They sold their land and the things they owned. Then they divided the money and gave it to those people who needed it. ⁴⁶The believers met together in the Temple every day. They all had the same purpose. They broke bread in their homes, happy to share their food with joyful hearts. ⁴⁷They praised God, and all the people liked them. More and more people were being saved every day; the Lord was adding those people to the group of believers.

More ➠

From Acts 2

? What were some of the things the new believers did?

? How did they feel about sharing their money and food?

? Fellowship means the getting together of two or more people who share similar beliefs or feelings. Christians experience this in a special way because they believe in Jesus. Think of all the ways that Christians have fellowship together. How many can you list? (Examples: Sunday school class, church dinners, having someone over to your house, etc.)

Lord, help me to share myself with other Christians. Show me ways to encourage others and give me ideas to help them get closer to You. Amen.

. . . You should meet together and encourage each other. Do this even more as you see the Day coming.
Hebrews 10:25b

CALL A SPECIAL MEETING OF THE CKC (SEE PAGE 40) FOR THE PURPOSE OF HAVING FELLOWSHIP. ASSIGN SOMEONE TO READ A BIBLE VERSE, SOMEONE TO TELL THE GROUP ABOUT SOMETHING SPECIAL GOD DID, AND SOMEONE TO SAY A PRAYER. TELL EVERYONE TO BRING SOMETHING GOOD TO EAT. THEN PLAN TO HAVE A GREAT TIME! ORGANIZE YOUR PLANS HERE.

Miracle at the Gate

ONE AFTERNOON WHEN PETER AND JOHN GO TO THE TEMPLE FOR PRAYER THEY FIND A LAME MAN BEGGING AT THE BEAUTIFUL GATE.

HAVE MERCY-- A COIN FOR THE POOR.

ONE day Peter and John **went to the Temple.** It was three o'clock in the afternoon. This was the time for the daily prayer service. ²There, at the Temple gate called Beautiful Gate, was a man who had been crippled all his life. Every day he was carried to this gate to beg. He would ask for money from the people going into the Temple. ³The man saw Peter and John going into the Temple and asked them for money. ⁴Peter and John looked straight at him and said, "Look at us!" ⁵The man looked at them; he thought they were going to give him some money. ⁶But Peter said, "I don't have any silver or gold, but I do have something else I can give you: By the power of Jesus Christ from Nazareth—stand up and walk!" ⁷Then Peter took the man's right hand and lifted him up. Immediately the man's feet and ankles became strong. ⁸He jumped up, stood on his feet, and began to walk. He went into the Temple with them, walking and jumping, and praising God.

⁹⁻¹⁰All the people recognized him. They knew he was the crippled man who always sat by the Beautiful Gate begging for money. Now they saw this same man walking and praising God. The people were amazed. They could not understand how this could happen.

From Acts 3

I HAVE NO MONEY, BUT I'LL GIVE YOU WHAT I HAVE. IN THE NAME OF JESUS CHRIST, RISE UP AND WALK!

More⁣⧫

? What did the crippled man expect to get from Peter and John? What did they give him instead?

? What did the man do when he was able to walk?

? When we praise God we are expressing words of thanks and love to Him. Think of five things that you can thank God for.

Lord, thank You for always being there to watch over me and provide for my needs. Help me to praise You in all that I do. Amen.

Let everything that breathes praise the Lord. Praise the Lord!

Psalm 150:6

WE CAN PRAISE GOD BY TELLING HIM WHAT A GREAT GOD HE IS. PRETEND THAT THIS SPACE IS A POSTER. WRITE WORDS OR PHRASES THAT DESCRIBE HOW YOU FEEL ABOUT GOD. SOME EXAMPLES ARE: YOU'RE A GREAT GOD! SUPER! PRAISE THE LORD!

155

To Preach or Not To Preach

WHILE Peter and John

were speaking to the people, a group of men came up to them. There were Jewish priests, the captain of the soldiers that guarded the Temple, and some Sadducees. [2]They were upset because the two apostles were teaching the people. Peter and John were preaching that people will rise from death through the power of Jesus. [3]The Jewish leaders grabbed Peter and John and put them in jail. It was already night, so they kept them in jail until the next day. [4]But many of those who heard Peter and John preach believed the things they said. There were now about 5,000 men in the group of believers.

YOU ARE UNDER ARREST!

[5]The next day the Jewish leaders, the older Jewish leaders, and the teachers of the law met in Jerusalem. [6]Annas the high priest, Caiaphas, John, and Alexander were there. Everyone from the high priest's family was there. [7]They made Peter and John stand before them. The Jewish leaders asked them: "By what power or authority did you do this?"

[8]Then Peter was filled with the Holy Spirit. He said to them, "Rulers of the people and you older leaders, [9]are you questioning us about a good thing that was done to a crippled man? Are you asking us who made him well? [10]We want all of you and all the Jewish people to know that this man was made well by the power of Jesus Christ from Nazareth!

. . . [12]Jesus is the only One who can save people. His name is the only power in the world that has been given to save people. And we must be saved through him!"

[13]The Jewish leaders saw that Peter and John were not afraid to speak. They understood that these men had no special training or education. So they were amazed. Then they realized that Peter and John had been with Jesus. [14]They saw the crippled man standing there beside the two apostles. They saw that the man was healed. So they could say nothing against them . . . .

[18]They told them not to speak or to teach at all in the name of Jesus. [19]But Peter and John answered them, "What do you think is right? What would God want? Should we obey you or God? [20]We cannot keep quiet. We must speak about what we have seen and heard."

156

From Acts 4

THE NEXT MORNING THEY ARE BROUGHT BEFORE THE SANHEDRIN, THE SAME JEWISH COURT THAT CONDEMNED JESUS TO DEATH. BESIDE THEM-- PERFECTLY WELL-- STANDS THE MAN WHO HAD BEEN LAME FROM BIRTH.

BY WHAT POWER AND IN WHOSE NAME HAVE YOU HEALED THIS MAN?

? Why did the group of men put Peter and John in jail?

? God wanted Peter and John to preach to people who needed to know Jesus, yet they had to go through some bad things. What did they experience?

WHETHER IT IS RIGHT IN THE EYES OF GOD FOR US TO OBEY HIM OR YOU, YOU MUST DECIDE. BUT WE HAVE TO KEEP ON PREACHING WHAT WE HAVE SEEN AND HEARD.

? It takes courage to stand up for what is right, and sometimes in doing that we may have to go through some tough stuff ourselves. Think of a time when you told the truth about something and because of doing so received bad treatment from others. An example: because of your honesty some kids at school wouldn't speak to you, or maybe you had to face a punishment.

Lord, give me the courage to stand up for what's right, regardless of the consequences. Help me to remember that no matter how bad things look, You are in control of my life and You are always there by my side. Amen.

So do not lose the courage that you had in the past. It has a great reward. You must hold on, so you can do what God wants and receive what he has promised.

Hebrews 10:35, 36

157

SOMETIMES IT'S HARD TO HAVE COURAGE BECAUSE YOU FEEL ALL ALONE. DRAW A PICTURE OF YOU. THEN DRAW A PICTURE OF JESUS STANDING RIGHT BESIDE YOU. REMEMBER THAT GOD IS ALWAYS THERE TO GIVE YOU THE COURAGE YOU NEED FOR ANY SITUATION.

Honesty

A **man named Ananias and his wife Sapphira sold some land.** 2But he gave only part of the money to the apostles. He secretly kept some of it for himself. His wife knew about this, and she agreed to it. 3Peter said, "Ananias, why did you let Satan rule your heart? You lied to the Holy Spirit. Why did you keep part of the money you received for the land for yourself? 4Before you sold the land, it belonged to you. And even after you sold it, you could have used the money any way you wanted. Why did you think of doing this? You lied to God, not to men!" 5-6When Ananias heard this, he fell down and died. Some young men came in, wrapped up his body, carried it out, and buried it. And everyone who heard about this was filled with fear.

7About three hours later his wife came in. She did not know what had happened. 8Peter said to her, "Tell me how much money you got for your field. Was it this much?"

Sapphira answered, "Yes, that was the price."

9Peter said to her, "Why did you and your husband agree to test the Spirit of the Lord? Look! The men who buried your husband are at the door! They will carry you out." 10At that moment Sapphira fell down by his feet and died. The young men came in and saw that she was dead. They carried her out and buried her beside her husband. 11The whole church and all the others who heard about these things were filled with fear.

From Acts 5

? What did Ananias and Sapphira agree to do?

? Did they have to give all the money to the church? (See verse 4.)

? Sometimes we are more interested in how things look to others than we are in being honest. Sure, they sold their land and gave money to the church, but they wanted Peter to think that they gave ALL the money. Jeff wants his mom to think that he's spent hours on his homework, when really he spent most of the time in his room reading the comics. Is this honest? Why or why not?

Dear God,
show me ways to be
more honest with the people
around me. Help me to check myself
every day to make sure that my life follows
the example You gave me.   Amen.

The honest person will live safely. But the one who is dishonest will be caught.

Proverbs 10:9

THINK FOR A MOMENT ABOUT HOW HONEST YOU HAVE BEEN LATELY WITH YOUR FRIENDS, YOUR TEACHERS, AND YOUR FAMILY. WHAT IS ONE WAY THAT YOU COULD IMPROVE IN THIS AREA? WRITE DOWN YOUR PLAN IN A PRAYER TO GOD.

DEAR GOD:

DEDICATED TO THE RIGHT CAUSE

IN **Jerusalem Saul was still trying to frighten the followers of the Lord by saying he would kill them.** So he went to the high priest ²and asked him to write letters to the synagogues in the city of Damascus. Saul wanted the high priest to give him the authority to find people in Damascus who were followers of Christ's Way. If he found any there, men or women, he would arrest them and bring them back to Jerusalem.

³So Saul went to Damascus. As he came near the city, a bright light from heaven suddenly flashed around him. ⁴Saul fell to the ground. He heard a voice saying to him, "Saul, Saul! Why are you doing things against me?"

⁵Saul said, "Who are you, Lord?"

The voice answered, "I am Jesus. I am the One you are trying to hurt. ⁶Get up now and go into the city. Someone there will tell you what you must do."

⁷The men traveling with Saul stood there, but they said nothing. They heard the voice, but they saw no one. ⁸Saul got up from the ground. He opened his eyes, but he could not see. So the men with Saul took his hand and led him into Damascus.

IN TIME PAUL BECOMES THE MOST BRILLIANT PUPIL OF THE FAMOUS TEACHER, GAMALIEL. TOGETHER THEY DISCUSS THE SCRIPTURES-- ESPECIALLY THE PARTS THAT TELL ABOUT THE COMING OF THE SAVIOR.

LIKE KING DAVID, HE WILL MAKE OUR COUNTRY STRONG AND POWERFUL. IF ONLY HE WOULD COME NOW-- I'D SPEND MY LIFE SERVING HIM.

PAUL, WHAT'S THE MATTER?

MY EYES—I CAN'T SEE! HELP ME INTO THE CITY.

161

[9]For three days Saul could not see, and he did not eat or drink.
[10]There was a follower of Jesus in Damascus named
Ananias. The Lord spoke to Ananias in a vision, "Ananias!"
Ananias answered, "Here I am, Lord."
[11]The Lord said to him, "Get up and go to the street called
Straight Street. Find the house of Judas. Ask for a man named
Saul from the city of Tarsus. He is there now, praying. [12]Saul
has seen a vision. In it a man named Ananias comes to him
and lays his hands on him. Then he sees again."
[13]But Ananias answered, "Lord, many people have told me
about this man and the terrible things he did to your people
in Jerusalem. [14]Now he has come here to Damascus. The
leading priests have given him the power to arrest everyone
who worships you."
[15]But the Lord said to Ananias, "Go! I have chosen Saul for
an important work. He must tell about me to non-Jews, to
kings, and to the people of Israel. [16]I will show him how
much he must suffer for my name." *From Acts 9*

? Why did Saul want to find Jesus' followers in
  Damascus?

? After Saul became a Christian, how did he act toward
  Christians?

? A dedicated person is one who goes after something
  with his or her whole heart. Saul was dedicated to
  killing Christians because he felt strongly that that was
  the right thing to do. Name some areas where a person
  can be dedicated. Some examples are: sports, music,
  being a minister or a teacher, etc.

Dear God, help me to stay dedicated to the right cause—serving You. Thank You for Your Word that can help me to keep on track and not get into areas that wouldn't please You. Amen.

So brothers, since God has shown us great mercy, I beg you to offer your lives as a living sacrifice to him. Your offering must be only for God and pleasing to him.

Romans 12:1

PAUL WAS DEDICATED TO THE WRONG CAUSE WHEN HE KILLED THE CHRISTIANS. BUT WHEN JESUS SPOKE TO HIM ON THE ROAD TO DAMASCUS, HE BECAME DEDICATED TO THE RIGHT CAUSE--HELPING PEOPLE BECOME CHRISTIANS. HOW CAN YOU BECOME MORE DEDICATED TO JESUS? THINK OF TWO THINGS YOU COULD DO WITH YOUR WHOLE HEART TO SHOW GOD THAT YOU MEAN BUSINESS!

1.

2.

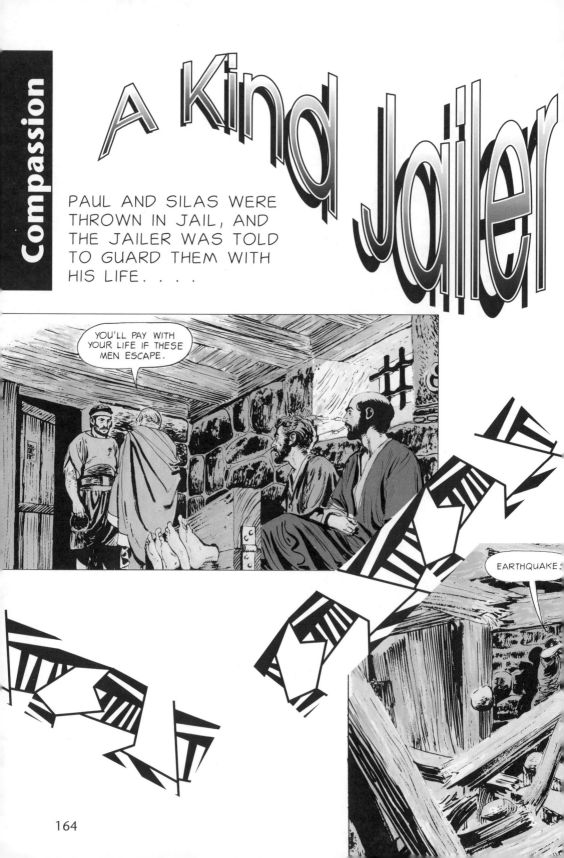

THEY'RE GONE! I MIGHT AS WELL KILL MYSELF.

NO! NO! WE'RE ALL HERE!

ABOUT midnight Paul and Silas **were praying and singing** songs to God.

The other prisoners were listening to them. 26Suddenly, there was a big earthquake. It was so strong that it shook the foundation of the jail. Then all the doors of the jail broke open. All the prisoners were freed from their chains. 27The jailer woke up and saw that the jail doors were open. He thought that the prisoners had already escaped. So he got his sword and was about to kill himself. 28But Paul shouted, "Don't hurt yourself! We are all here!"

29The jailer told someone to bring a light. Then he ran inside. Shaking with fear, he fell down before Paul and Silas. 30Then he brought them outside and said, "Men, what must I do to be saved?"

31They said to him, "Believe in the Lord Jesus and you will be saved—you and all the people in your house." 32So Paul and Silas told the message of the Lord to the jailer and all the people in his house. 33At that hour of the night the jailer took Paul and Silas and washed their wounds. Then he and all his people were baptized immediately. 34After this the jailer took Paul and Silas home and gave them food. He and his family were very happy because they now believed in God.

From Acts 16

WHAT MUST I DO TO BE SAVED?

BELIEVE ON THE LORD JESUS CHRIST.

? What happened at midnight that made the jailer afraid?

? What was the jailer's reaction to what Paul and Silas told him?

? When the jailer heard about Jesus, it changed his life. He changed from a hardened jailer to a man full of compassion. He washed Paul and Silas's wounds and took them home and gave them food. The more we know about Jesus, the more we want to help others. Think of a time when you helped someone who was in need.

More ⟹ 165

Lord, thank You for always caring about the needs of people. Use me to show compassion to those who need help so that they see Your love through the way I act toward them. Amen.

My children, our love should not be only words and talk. Our love must be true love. And we should show that love by what we do.

I John 3:18

WHEN GOD'S LOVE FILLS OUR HEART, WE WANT TO DO NICE THINGS FOR PEOPLE. WE FEEL COMPASSION FOR PEOPLE IN TROUBLE AND WANT TO HELP THEM. THINK OF SOMEONE IN YOUR CHURCH OR NEIGHBORHOOD WHO COULD REALLY USE SOME HELP (MAYBE THEY NEED CHEERING UP OR THEIR YARD RAKED OR THEIR PLANTS WATERED). ASK GOD TO SHOW YOU WAYS TO HELP THAT PERSON AND THEN OFFER YOUR HELP. WRITE YOUR IDEAS HERE.

1.

2.

3.

4.

5.

Perseverence

"**I have been in prison. . .** I have been hurt . . . in beatings. I have been near death many times [24]Five times the Jews have given me their punishment of 39 lashes with a whip. [25]Three different times I was beaten with rods. One time they tried to kill me with stones. Three times I was in ships that were wrecked, and one of these times I spent the night and the next day in the sea. [26]I have gone on many travels. And I have been in danger from rivers, from thieves, from my own people, the Jews, and from those who are not Jews. I have been in danger in cities, in places where no one lives, and on the sea. . . . [27]I have done hard and tiring work, and many times I did not sleep. I have been hungry and thirsty. Many times I have been without food. I have been cold and without clothes."

From II Corinthians 11

"**My life is being given as an offering to God.** The time has come for me to leave this life. [7]I have fought the good fight. I have finished the race. I have kept the faith. [8]Now, a crown is waiting for me. I will get that crown for being right with God. The Lord is the judge who judges rightly, and he will give me the crown on that Day. He will give that crown not only to me but to all those who have waited with love for him to come again."

From II Timothy 4

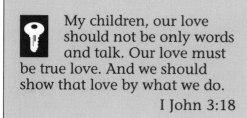

IN ANGER THE PEOPLE TURN AGAINST PAUL. A MOB DRAGS HIM FROM THE TEMPLE AND STARTS TO BEAT HIM.

LOOK OUT-- ROMAN SOLDIERS ARE COMING!

Finishing the Race

Morell

? Did Paul live an easy life because he was a Christian? How do you know?

? What was Paul's attitude about the life he had lived? (See II Timothy 4:6.) Did he complain to God?

? Paul used the illustration of finishing a race to talk about the end of his life. When you think of running a race, what are some things that happen that make you want to stop running?

God is working in you to help you want to do what pleases him. Then he gives you the power to do it.

Philippians 2:13

Lord, help me to keep following You and obeying Your Word no matter what happens in my life. Thanks, God, for giving me the strength to keep trying. Amen.

PAUL'S GOAL WAS TO RECEIVE A CROWN THAT THE LORD WOULD GIVE HIM IN HEAVEN. IT IS IMPORTANT FOR US TO KEEP OUR GOAL IN MIND. THEN WHEN PROBLEMS COME, WE CAN REMEMBER THAT GOD HAS PREPARED A GREAT REWARD FOR US IN HEAVEN. DRAW A PICTURE OF YOURSELF RUNNING TOWARD A FINISH LINE WHERE A BEAUTIFUL CROWN WAITS FOR YOU.